SHAKESPEARE IN ITALY

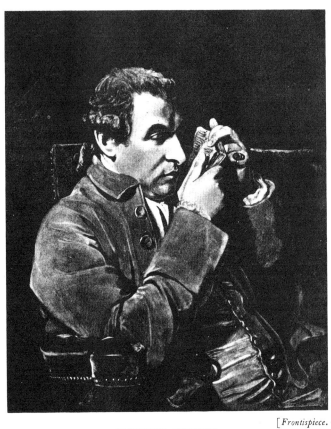

[*Frontispiece.*

GIUSEPPE BARETTI.
(From the painting by Sir Joshua Reynolds.)

SHAKESPEARE IN ITALY

BY

LACY COLLISON-MORLEY

BENJAMIN BLOM
New York

First published 1916
Reissued 1967 by
Benjamin Blom, Inc. New York 10452
Library of Congress Cat. Card No. 67-23862

Prefatory Note

Portions of this book have already appeared elsewhere —'An Italian "Hamlet" in the Eighteenth Century' in the *Athenæum*, 'Shakespear in Italy' in the *Contemporary Review* and 'Baretti, Johnson and Shakespeare' in the *Times Literary Supplement*.

My best thanks for kind assistance are due, among others, to Signor Diego Angeli, Signorina Laura Lattes, Senator Guido Mazzoni and above all to my friend, Professor Luigi Piccioni.

From an interesting article on 'Shakespeare e la Musica' in the *Nuova Antologia* for April 16, 1916, by Margherita Berio, it appears that Salieri composed an opera entitled 'Falstaff' in Vienna as early as 1798. The name of the librettist is not given.

June, 1916.   L. C.-M.

Contents

PAGE

PREFATORY NOTE vii

I BEFORE VOLTAIRE 1

II VOLTAIRE AND HIS FOLLOWERS . . 15

III ANGLOMANIA AND MORE FAVOURABLE
JUDGMENTS 30

IV SHAKESPEARE IN ITALY FROM 1790 TO
1800 62

V SHAKESPEARE AND THE ITALIAN STAGE
BEFORE 1800 79

VI SHAKESPEARE IN ITALY DURING THE
NAPOLEONIC PERIOD (1800–15) . 83

VII SHAKESPEARE IN ITALY DURING THE
ROMANTIC MOVEMENT (1815–30) . 98

VIII LATER ITALIAN TRANSLATIONS OF SHAKE-
SPEARE 134

IX SHAKESPEARE AND THE LATER ROMANTIC
DRAMA IN ITALY 139

X SHAKESPEARE ON THE ITALIAN STAGE
DURING THE NINETEENTH CENTURY 151

APPENDIX 165

BIBLIOGRAPHY 166

INDEX 175

ILLUSTRATIONS

GIUSEPPE BARETTI—From the painting by Sir
Joshua Reynolds in Holland House, Ken-
sington . . . . . . *Frontispiece*

FACING PAGE

SAVERIO BETTINELLI—From the frontispiece to
Vol. I of his Collected Works, Venezia,
1799–1801 21

TITLE-PAGE OF DOMENICO VALENTINI'S TRANS-
LATION OF *Julius Cæsar* 39

ALESSANDRO VERRI—From the engraving by C.
Rampoldi in Vol. I of his selected works
in the 'Classici Italiani', Milano, 1822 . 56

THE SALON OF GIUSTINA RENIER-MICHIEL—
From the engraving of Tommaso Viola's
drawing in Luigi Carrer's *Anello di Sette
Gemme*, Venezia, 1838 77

ALESSANDRO MANZONI 112

GIULIO CARCANO—From the bust outside the
door of the Brera Library, Milan . . 137

ERNESTO ROSSI AS 'HAMLET' . . . 155

SHAKESPEARE IN ITALY

I

BEFORE VOLTAIRE

ITALIAN visitors, ecclesiastical and others, were common in England down to the Reformation and throughout the sixteenth century they were still to be found in considerable numbers, since Italy and England were bound together by important commercial interests. During the seventeenth century, however, there was a great falling off. Already suspect on account of her religion, England became something more with the triumph of Puritanism. The execution of Charles I sent a thrill of horror through Europe. Gregorio Leti, who embraced the reformed religion, remarks in his *Teatro Britanico*, I. 8 and II. 1, 3, that there were far more English families in Venice and Leghorn than Italians in England. The Restoration did something to revive interest in this country on the continent, but the Huguenots who flocked here after the Revocation of the Edict of Nantes (1685), and still more after the Revolution three years later, sowed the first seeds of that cosmopolitanism in literature which was to characterize the eighteenth century. In reviews such as the *Bibliothèque Angloise* (Amsterdam, 1717–28), and the *Journal Britannique* (The Hague, 1733–47), published by the French refugees with the avowed purpose of

B

spreading a knowledge of England and all things English among their countrymen, we find the germ of that French Anglomania which was ultimately to familiarize Italy and, indeed, the whole of the continent with the literature of the North.[1]

But Italians who had the opportunity of seeing England for themselves were fully able to appreciate us without waiting for France to show them the way. The famous Florentine physician Antonio Cocchi, who came to England with Lord Huntingdon in 1723, wrote to the Marchese Scaramuccia Visconti (4 April, 1727): 'A man who has spent some time there is spoilt for ever, unless he settles there. I have philosophised enough upon this subject and have adduced facts and reasons in support of my opinion. . . . Everyone who has once enjoyed that country seems to me to feel the same about it, even the Marchese Fiaschi, who did not have a very pleasant time there. You cannot live happily anywhere else. Not a bed, not a table, not a house, not a city, not a people but reminds you of that fortunate isle. Oh, that I were the Marchese Visconti!'

But English literature was slow in crossing the Alps. In his *Teatro Britanico*, already mentioned, which was published in London in 1683, Gregorio Leti says that our 'splendid and magnificent theatres deserve to be seen by foreigners . . . for all that concerns the scenes of the comedies, the skill of the actors, the inventions

---

[1] J. **Texte,** *Jean-Jacques Rousseau et Les Origines du Cosmopolitisme Littéraire,* chap. i. section 3.

and designs and everything else; they are in advance of the other theatres of Europe.' But of the plays and playwrights he tells us nothing. He knew that his countrymen took no interest in our literature. Probably he took none himself. In any case he did not think it worth discussing.

Among the few Italians of quality who travelled to England at this time was Cosimo, son of Ferdinand II, Grand Duke of Tuscany. He came to England in 1669, bringing with him Lorenzo Magalotti (1637–1712). Magalotti, with his encyclopædic, if rather superficial, culture, belonged to the eighteenth rather than to the seventeenth century. Science and philosophy were his chief preoccupations and he was elected a Fellow of the Royal Society. But he was also a man of letters. He made several long stays in England in the service of the Tuscan court, and a reference in a letter to the paper on Ladies' Fans proves that he lived to read the *Spectator* as it came out. In any case he appears to have been the first Italian to take an interest in our literature. His version of John Philips's *Cider* was not published till 1749, when scientific poetry was all the rage, but he is also the author of an unpublished version of the *Splendid Shilling*. He even attempted to translate the first book of *Paradise Lost*, turning his attention to Waller's *Battle of the Summer Isles* when the task proved too much for him.[1] Such a man would, of course, frequent the theatre in London, and Graf assures us that he 'certainly knew something of Shakespeare'.[2]

[1] S. Fermi, *Lorenzo Magalotti.*   [2] *Anglomania*, p. 313.

But the best proof of the absolute ignorance of Shakespeare that prevailed on the other side of the Alps during the early years of the eighteenth century is the fact that a man of Apostolo Zeno's vast learning could write a music-drama, *Ambleto*, without ever having heard of *Hamlet*. Printed in 1705, it was produced at the San Casciano Theatre in Venice in the following year, with music by Francesco Gasperini. An English version of this opera was even given at the Haymarket Theatre in 1712. Zeno has gone to Saxo Grammaticus for his story, but he has introduced some strange variations to bring it into line with the requirements of the lyric stage. The characters are :—

Ambleto, in love with Veremonda.

Veremonda, Princess of Albania, in love with Ambleto.

Fengone, the usurping King, also in love with Veremonda.

Gerilda, the Queen, who has unwillingly married her husband's murderer.

Ildegarde, a Danish Princess, who, besides being in love with Ambleto, has played a part in Fengone's past.

Valdemaro, the conqueror of Albania, also in love with Veremonda.

Siffrido, Captain of the King's guard.

Ambleto knows that the King has murdered his father, Orvendillo, and therefore pretends madness to allay suspicion. Valdemaro asks for Veremonda's hand as a reward for his victory, but she begs the King not

to give her to her country's conqueror. He readily
consents and proposes to make Ildegarde Valdemaro's
wife, but they agree to leave each other free. The
King suspects Ambleto's designs and puts him to the
three tests recorded by Saxo. First he is left with
Veremonda, but she warns him that the King is watching
him in hiding by writing on the ground with a spear.
Then the King decides to go away, leaving the Queen
as regent during his absence, after ordering a faithful
guard to remain in hiding in the Queen's apartments
and listen to any talk she may have with Ambleto.
But Siffrido betrays this design to Ambleto, who kills
the guard before speaking to his mother. The interview is the one scene in the play at all like Shakespeare,
both scenes being based on Saxo.

Suddenly Siffrido enters and tells Ambleto that
Valdemaro has carried off Veremonda. Ambleto over-
takes him and tells him that he is only feigning
madness. He pardons Valdemaro's offence and com-
mands his obedience. Valdemaro goes. The King finds
Ambleto with Veremonda and remarks that a man who
has sense enough to go off with Veremonda is not so
very mad, after all. But Valdemaro explains matters
and is pardoned, since he is too powerful to punish.

In Act iii the King decides to repudiate his wife
and marry Veremonda, telling her that Ambleto's life,
which is forfeit for the slaying of the guard, depends
on her answer. Ambleto bids her consent, as he is
nearly ready to act. He next enters dressed as Bacchus
with a chorus. A cup is offered him, but he dashes it

to the ground, having been warned by Siffrido that it is poisoned. Then he himself brings in a second cup for the King, who drains it and goes off with the shrinking Veremonda. But the wine is so heavily drugged that he falls into a deep sleep before he can consummate the marriage and wakes to find himself in chains. He is hurried off to execution and all ends happily.

The first Italian to mention Shakespeare is Antonio Conti of Padua (1677–1749), in a letter to Jacopo Martelli, prefixed to his own play, *Il Cesare* (Faenza, 1726). He was in London from 1715 to 1718, where he realized the dream of every cultivated Italian by making the acquaintance of Newton, among other people of distinction and position. But like William III he was driven to 'Kinsington' by asthma. Here he met John Sheffield, Duke of Buckinghamshire, who showed him his tragedies of *Cæsar* and *Brutus*, 'which are only Sasper's [*sic*] cut into two'. 'Sasper', he proceeds, 'is the Corneille of the English, only far more irregular than Corneille, though, like him, he is full of great ideas and noble sentiments. I shall only mention his *Cæsar* here. Sasper makes him die in the third act. The rest of the tragedy is taken up with Mark Antony's speech to the People, then with the wars and the deaths of Cassius and Brutus. Could there be a greater violation of the unities of time, action and place? But the English, before *Cato*, treat Aristotle's rules with contempt, for the aim of tragedy is to please, and the best is the one which is most successful in this. . . .

Such were, I imagine, the views of most Italians, spoilt by Spanish comedies, in the seventeenth century.' He is surprised that no one thought of translating the English plays of the time, since 'they are crowded with incident, like the Spanish, while their characters are certainly more natural and more pleasing.' The histories especially he thinks might have proved most instructive to his countrymen then. (*Il Cesare*, p. 54.)

Conti's own tragedy was planned in London, but the scheme was much changed when he came to write it in Paris. The unities are, of course, strictly observed and it ends with Cæsar's murder. But for his introductory letter, it would probably not have occurred to anyone to imagine that Conti had ever heard of Shakespeare, or even of Buckinghamshire. There is not a trace of Shakespearean art, or a hint of an anticipation of romanticism to be found anywhere in the play. Indeed, how could there be at this period? Yet it is not unlikely that the choice of the subject was due to Conti's visit to London. Moreover, in his tragedy, as in Shakespeare's, Cassius's attempts to win over Brutus form the most noteworthy incident of the first act. It is, of course, possible that this is due to Sheffield's influence, but there is no need to go beyond Plutarch for the idea. 'In Conti,' says Colagrosso,[1] 'we have, so to speak, the skeletons of some scenes from Shakespeare, but not a spark of the life that animates them. Again, it is Calpurnia's dream that dominates the fourth act of Conti's *Cesare*, and Colagrosso, who

[1] *La Prima Tragedia di Ant. Conti*, p. 21.

rightly considers these scenes among the best in the tragedy, is of opinion that he owes them to Shakespeare. It is true that Calpurnia does not appear at all in Sheffield's plays, but Conti makes far more of her than did Shakespeare. Are we not once more justified in regarding Plutarch as the common source for both poets? Conti's notes to his translation of the *Rape of the Lock*, which was completed as early as 1721 or 1722, though not published till 1740, are usually well-informed. Yet on the lines,

> Not fierce Othello in so loud a strain
> Stormed for the handkerchief that caused his pain.

he remarks that 'the allusion is to a passage in an English tragedy'.[1] Is this not sufficient proof that Conti did not know the name of the author of *Othello*? This fact, combined with his spelling of the poet's name, can surely be taken as conclusive evidence that he knew nothing of Shakespeare except what he had picked up in talk with Buckinghamshire and possibly other English friends.

'*Cato* is the first regular tragedy of the English', proceeds Conti, thus anticipating Voltaire, just as he was the first to call Shakespeare the English Corneille. And he goes on to praise Addison's tragedy with an enthusiasm which would have satisfied his warmest admirers and which was soon to be echoed by the leading men of letters throughout Europe.

---

[1] This note is repeated almost *verbatim* in Bonducci's translation of the poem. (Naples, 1761.)

Very different is the tone of Paolo Rolli (1687–1765), the first of his countrymen to understand and appreciate Shakespeare. Like Conti he came to England in 1715, where he wrote operas for Handel and taught the Royal Family and select members of the English aristocracy Italian. He was one of the best Italian lyric poets of his day, and his work owes not a little to his stay in this country. In the Life of Milton, prefixed to his translation of *Paradise Lost*, for which Pope placed him in the *Dunciad*, he tells us that Shakespeare was 'an English gentleman who, in Queen Elizabeth's reign, raised the English theatre to heights which can never be surpassed by means of his tragedies.' The fact that he had not received a regular education only proves how prodigious was his genius, though Rolli refuses to believe that he did not even know Latin. Like Conti, he praises the histories and considers that other nations would do well to imitate them. He compares Shakespeare with Dante and says that the coarseness in his plays must be ascribed to the actors, 'who added of their own accord whatever they felt or knew by experience would please the crowd.' Rolli is obviously quite familiar with Shakespeare. He knows that *Othello* is derived from Giraldi Cintio. In his *Remarks upon M. Voltaire's Essay on the Epick Poetry of the European Nations* (1728), he refers to *Henry IV* and *Richard III*, and declares that 'what will make Shakespeare shine for ever upon the British stage is the strength of painting in the characters of the English and Roman great men he sets forth in his historical tragedies, so lively represented in their vertues, tempers and faults that they still seem to live.' He also points out that Voltaire ' has never seen or read the tragedy of *Macbeth*, which to my taste is the best English tragedy, nor the *Tempest* of Shakespeare.' Though Rolli admits that an English friend had helped him in his work, there is no reason to suppose that his references to Shakespeare are not his own. It is a pity that on returning home with a fortune amassed in England he did not devote his leisure to introducing our literature to his country-men instead of composing the scurrilous libels on the land which had treated him so well that were found among his papers after his death.

But occasional allusions to Shakespeare by men who had lived long in England did nothing to make him known in Italy, where they would pass quite unnoticed. Some far more powerful stimulus was needed to awaken interest in a literature, and above all in a drama, so utterly opposed to all the traditions of the day. Not that there was any lack of enthusiasm for tragedy among men of culture in the peninsula. Never had there been such a fever of tragedy-writing, inspired largely by a desire to rival the great French poets. For Italy had never produced a great tragic poet, much less a great national drama. Yet there was no attempt at reform. The growth of French influence, which had altogether superseded that of Spain by the end of the seventeenth century, continued undiminished during the eighteenth. Italian writers could devise no better way of accomplishing their ambition than to follow in

the footsteps of the men they were trying to rival.
Martelli, considering that Italy's want of success in
tragedy was due to her not possessing a suitable metre,
adopted one which has come to be known as 'versi
martelliani', though it is as old as Ciullo d'Alcamo. He
meant it to produce the same effect as the Alexandrine,
which it closely resembles, but he was not imitated.
The unrhymed hendecasyllable superseded all others
as the recognized vehicle for tragic poetry. This might
have been expected to make Shakespeare appeal more
readily to the Italian ear than to the French, which
was used to the Alexandrine. It is an especial favourite
with Fletcher. *The Wild Goose Chase* is almost entirely
composed in it. But tragedy was not popular in Italy
and was rarely acted, except by learned academies. The
authors were generally men of learning, wholly unin-
spired, and their work was not calculated to break
down the prevailing prejudice. Scipione Maffei's once
famous *Merope* (1713), was the only tragedy of note that
resulted from these efforts. Maffei visited England,
where he was made much of, but all he has to say of
Shakespeare, in his *Saggio delle Traduzioni Italiane*, is that
he was 'one of the sources of noble English poetry.'

Still, it is noteworthy that the two really original
dramatic writers of the time were at heart rebels.
Metastasio was the one great poet of the day. The
music-drama, which he perfected, had come into existence after Aristotle, and was therefore exempted from
the rules. Dr. Johnson claimed the same privilege for
Shakespeare's historical plays on the same grounds.

But Metastasio went much further. In a letter to Ranieri dei Calzabigi (16 February, 1754), who was then in Paris, he says that he had felt it his duty to read every important play written, not only in Greek, Latin and Italian, but also in French and Spanish. 'I remedied my ignorance of English by existing translations, in order to discover, so far as I could without knowing the language, the progress made by the theatre in that country.' Since La Place's analyses and translations of Shakespeare had begun to appear in 1746, Metastasio almost certainly read them, though he nowhere mentions Shakespeare, and the only English influence which can be traced in his work is that of Addison's *Cato*. Another letter of the same year (15 October), shows him trying to induce Calzabigi to moderate the tone of some remarks he seems to have been about to publish 'against the half-educated, both French and Italian'. He says that his (Metastasio's) opinions upon the unities and the chorus would come better from Calzabigi's mouth than from his own, since he was an interested party. But the question deserved serious discussion, especially in France, where 'there has been a desire to fetter the poor theatre with a rigour which has no justification in any poetic canon of an ancient master and against which numberless instances can be adduced, both Greek and Latin'; and he proceeds to give some. Metastasio was never remarkable for moral courage and his *Estratto dell' Arte Poetica di Aristotele* was not published till after his death. In this he protests against the narrow modern interpretation of the *Poetics*, carefully tabulating all the instances of the violation of the unities in the Greek and Latin drama, and discusses the absurdities of the restrictions they impose. When the attempt is justified by success, he considers it highly praiseworthy for a vigorous genius to break the bonds of authority and custom. Otherwise the first efforts of an art would be the last signal of our hopes, 'and all the immense portion of the world beyond the Pillars of Hercules would, so far as we are concerned, have been created to no purpose.'

Similarly Goldoni, the only great Italian writer of comedies, ably attacks the unity of Place in his *Teatro Comico*,[1] and has plenty to say against the unities in general in the dedication of his *Malcontenti*, with which we shall deal later. But he never reprinted this dedication in later editions of his plays, and in his Memoirs, written in French after he had settled in Paris, he states that he has observed the unities in all his comedies. But the observance is often more apparent than real.

Clearly, then, both Metastasio and Goldoni realized the futility of protesting in the prevailing state of public opinion. In Italy, as elsewhere in Europe, France was supreme in all questions of taste, and the unities were one of the first articles in her creed. Gallomania was, in fact, growing apace, though it did not reach its zenith till after the Peace of Aix-la-Chapelle in 1748, when Italy was at last free from foreign war and to a great extent from foreign dominion. 'It is they', says Goldoni

[1] See the translation of the passage on p. 143 of Mr. Chatfield-Taylor's *Goldoni*.

of the French in his Memoirs, 'who give the tone to the whole of Europe. . . . It is the French whom everyone is everywhere trying to imitate.' 'The library of men and women of the world is only French,' says Cesarotti, using a Gallicism, 'uomini di mondo', in his Italian. French was the language of polite society in Piedmont; when Alfieri began to train himself for writing tragedies he had to learn Italian almost as if it had been a foreign tongue. French theatrical companies were common in Turin, where Alfieri saw the principal French classical tragedies and comedies performed in 1765. Even Baretti, who cannot be accused of undue partiality for the French, considered that Italians of his day were 'as far below the French in literature, as the people of Morocco are below the Italians.' (*Frust. Let.*, No. 19.)

II

VOLTAIRE AND HIS FOLLOWERS

HENCE there was no chance of Shakespeare becoming known at all in Italy until he had aroused the interest of a Frenchman of sufficient standing in the world of letters to command attention. Muralt's appreciative and well-informed *Lettres sur les Anglais et les Français*, which were written in 1694–5, though not published till 1725, seem to have been no better known in Italy than l'Abbé Prévost's *Mémoires d'un Homme de Qualité* and *Le Pour et Le Contre*. But this gift of commanding attention was, as M. Jusserand remarks, pre-eminently possessed by Voltaire. Whatever he said, even though he merely repeated what others had said before him, was invariably listened to with the utmost respect, and nowhere more so than in Italy. 'It is common knowledge that our writers, with very few exceptions, prostrated themselves before Voltaire and it would be useless to add to the mass of evidence for this idolatry which has already been collected,' says Graf.[1] Hence his visit to England (1726–9), followed by the appearance of the *Lettres Philosophiques* in 1734, which mark an epoch in the history of Shakespeare in France, was the direct cause of his entering Italy. As so much of Italian opinion upon Shakespeare till the end of the

[1] *Anglomania*, p. 15.

century and beyond was derived from Voltaire we must mention the chief points of his criticism.

'Shakespeare, whom the English take for a Sophocles, flourished about the same time as Lope de Vega: he created the theatre; he possessed a genius forceful and fertile, natural and sublime, without a particle of good taste and without the least acquaintance with the rules. I am going to make an observation audacious, but true, that this author's merits have ruined the English theatre. There are scenes so fine, passages so great scattered through these monstrous farces called tragedies, that his pieces have always been played with the utmost success.' Consequently his eccentricities have come to be regarded as virtues after the lapse of two hundred years. Addison was the first Englishman to produce a 'reasonable tragedy', and Voltaire is astonished that an audience acquainted with *Cato* can endure such extravagances. Yet 'Shakespeare's brilliant monstrosities give a thousand times more pleasure than the wisdom of to-day. The genius of English poetry up to the present may be compared to a leafy tree planted by nature, throwing out at will a thousand branches, and growing irregularly, but strongly. It dies if you attempt to do violence to its nature and cut it like a tree in the garden of Marly.' Then follow contemptuous references to Othello strangling Desdemona and the gravediggers' scene in *Hamlet*, and the strange travesty of 'To be or not to be'. Voltaire had been more generous in his *Essay on Epic Poetry*. Referring to Shakespeare, he says of creative genius that 'it moves

forward without guide, without art, without rule. It
loses its way in its progress, but it leaves far behind it
all that can claim no other merit than reasonableness
and correctness.' In 1735 we first come across the 'Gille
de Foire'. In writing to M. de Cirey (3 November,
1735), and sending him the last scenes of his *Jules César*,
Voltaire describes them as a 'pretty faithful translation
of an English writer who lived about a hundred and
fifty years ago [no longer two hundred, be it observed]—
he is the Corneille of London, great madman everywhere else, more like Gille than Corneille ; but he has
some admirable passages.' It is noticeable that each
year Voltaire grows more contemptuous of the 'dunghill
that had fertilised a very ungrateful soil', to quote
Mrs. Montagu's well-known *mot*.

These were the texts upon which all Shakespearean
criticism was based not only in Italy, but throughout
Europe. Even Shakespeare's champions were not
ashamed to take their weapons from Voltaire's armoury.
The simile of the tree and the garden of Marly became
a commonplace with critics of both camps. Dr. Johnson
himself made use of it in the Preface to his edition.

Martin Sherlock was an enthusiastic admirer of
Shakespeare who travelled widely in Europe in 1779.
He even had the courage to defend him against Frederick
the Great in an intervew in Berlin. 'I should not have
said so much upon Shakespeare ', he writes in his *Fragment
on Shakespeare*, 'if from Paris to Berlin, from Berlin to
Naples I had not heard his name profaned. The words
monstrous farces and *gravediggers* have been repeated to

c

me in every town, and for a long time I could not conceive why everyone uttered precisely those two words and not a third. One day, happening to open a volume of Voltaire, the mystery was solved : the two words in question were found in that volume and all the critics had learned them by heart.' Sherlock was travelling nearly half a century after the words first appeared in print and it was almost half a century more before they had become meaningless.

The next mention of Shakespeare comes straight from the enemy's camp. Francesco Algarotti was perhaps the best known of the polished, cultivated *abati*, so characteristic of Italy at this time, who were welcome guests in the drawing-rooms of every capital in Europe, dabbling in everything and looking up to Voltaire as their master. Frederick the Great would hardly allow him out of his sight and made him a Count and a member of the Order of Merit. The letter to Franchini (22 October, 1735) which is usually printed before Voltaire's *Jules César* was actually written at Cirey, and Algarotti is obviously here acting as one of the great man's mouthpieces. 'In this tragedy', he says, 'Voltaire has set himself to imitate the severity of the English theatre, especially Shakespeare, in whom it is said, and rightly said, that there are "faults innumerable and thoughts inimitable." Of this his *Death of Julius Cæsar* is a proof. And you may well believe that our poet has taken from Shakespeare what Virgil took from Ennius. He has given in French the two last scenes of that tragedy which, when a few faults have been eliminated, are a perfect mirror of eloquence.' Voltaire has, in fact, adopted the severity, not the barbarity of the English stage.

By the following year Algarotti had actually seen *Julius Cæsar* in London, as we learn from Madame du Châtelet's letter to him dated 13 June, 1736. In 1757 he wrote to Muzio Spada (22 June), asking: 'What else could one imagine Brutus saying to the Roman People except, more or less, the words which Shakespeare puts into his mouth?' And he proceeds to give a prose translation of them. Algarotti had many English friends, and quotations from our poets, especially from Milton, are common in his letters. We find him writing to Paradisi (3 December, 1762), and complimenting Mason, whom he calls one of the first poets of our age, upon being such a philosopher as to imitate Shakespeare's virtues, but not his faults. Algarotti probably knew something of Shakespeare, but he was too complete a child of his age to be able to appreciate him.

Francesco Saverio Quadrio's *Della Storia e della Ragione d'Ogni Poesia* (Milan, 1743), Vol. I. p. 149, is the first Italian history of literature to mention Shakespeare, but the author merely transcribes Voltaire. 'In English theatres only plays like the Spanish were heard before the appearance of the celebrated Shakespeare, who was then looked upon almost as the Corneille of that nation. But although this poet possessed a fertile and vigorous genius and was endowed with a mind that combined the natural with the sublime, he had not, as M. de Voltaire says, the slightest acquaintance with the rules, nor are his poems anywhere illuminated by the light of good taste. Hence, instead of benefiting the English stage and correcting its defects, he brought it to utter ruin. Notwithstanding the fact that in his monstrous farces, called tragedies, there are some marvellous and beautiful scenes and some terrible and magnificent passages are to be found, these farces are outside the rules and altogether lacking in taste.' The Index volume (p. 213) contains a few additional biographical details and a little more abuse.

Quadrio is typical of Shakespeare's critics in Italy at this time, and we shall tabulate here the most important of the judgments which are derived directly from Voltaire. Luigi Riccoboni (the famous actor, Lelio) lived so long in Paris that it is perhaps hardly fair to class him as an Italian. He had, however, been in London and seen our theatres for himself. In his *Réflexions Historiques et Critiques*, which were written in 1734, though not printed till 1740, he says that 'English dramatic poets have drenched the stage in blood beyond belief,' and supports his statements by references to *Hamlet* and *Othello*, obviously borrowed from Voltaire. Moreover, the success of *Georges Barnewelt*, the first English play to be translated into French during the eighteenth century, as compared with that of *Cato*, proves that the national taste has not changed.

Carlo Denina's *Discorso sopra le Vicende della Letteratura* (1760), Vol. I. pp. 339-40, shows a little more knowledge, and the author at least had the originality to go to Voltaire's *Essay on Epic Poetry* for his more favourable

SPIRITUM PHEBUS TIBI, PHEBUS ARTEM
CARMINIS, NOMENQUE DEDIT POETÆ

[*To face p.* 21.

SAVERIO BETTINELLI.
(From the frontispiece to his Collected Works.)

opinion, though there is no sign of his having read
Shakespeare himself. He was a contemporary of Spenser,
we are told, 'with more grave faults, but greater and
more celebrated. When he began to write, Italian and
Spanish farces were the rage in England,' in spite of the
rules, which the critics never ceased to preach. 'Marlowe,
Shakespeare and Johnson created the English theatre on
these foundations. . . . Shakespeare knew no Greek and
perhaps hardly a little Latin and French. Having become
an actor by instinct, necessity, or whim, and having
proved himself superior to the others in ability, he was
made head of the troupe and then author of the plays
to be given, leaving the most learned far behind him,
one of the most remarkable instances of the superiority
of genius to art.'

The Jesuit Saverio Bettinelli (1718–1808), an enthusiastic Voltairian and, though less cosmopolitan, as
typical a representative of the literature of his day as
Algarotti, found the *Divina Commedia* sadly defective
when compared with the *Essay on Man*, and was, of
course, scandalized by Shakespeare. His *Lettere Inglesi*
abound in praise of a country which he had never seen,
and he envies Algarotti his long stay in the land 'of
art, of genius and of Newton.' 'It is true that Milton
is altogether English,' he says, 'that is, extreme in the
monstrosity and the sublimity of his poem. So also is
Shakespeare, so also are many others.' In an epigram
(*Opere*, Vol. XXII. p. 113), he says that Scespir—(this
is perhaps the cleverest of the Italian reproductions
of the sound of the name)—is an author wonderful,

immortal, divine, original, a great tragic poet; but
what are we to say of the taste that finds him so?

> Dirò con voi, Signore,
> Che Scespir è un autore
> Mirabile, immortale,
> Divino, originale,
> Gran tragico; ma poi,
> Che dir d'un gusto tale
> E che pensar di voi?

In his *Dialoghi sopra il Teatro Moderno* (1788) he is
more detailed, but not more original or more accurate.
Shakespeare is 'bestial, though sometimes sublime'.
He 'gives beer and brandy to his heroes in *Hamlet*,
makes Augustus, Antony, Lepidus, Pompey, Agrippa
and Mæcenas drink together and sing songs in chorus,
drunk as they are, in *Cleopatra*.' On the way to the
Capitol Cæsar invites the Senators to drink a bottle to
his health. In fact, though Bettinelli lived on into
Byron's day, he never wavered in his loyalty to the
poetic creed in which he had been brought up.

Melchiorre Cesarotti (1730–1808), though he owed
his fame largely to his translation of Ossian, fully shared
the views of his contemporaries upon Shakespeare. His
knowledge of English was limited, but he was certainly
acquainted with Le Tourneur and possibly with Shakespeare in the original. In his essay on Voltaire's *Jules
César* he tells us that Shakespeare's play is only a versified
story of the revolutions of Rome and should rather
have been called the Roman Republic. 'This drama has
no merit, either for invention or for skill in the regular

development of the plot. The one merit it does possess is the enthusiasm and fire of the style, and a sustained vividness, which not unfrequently degenerates into vulgarity. The productions of this rough and great genius are like the colossus of Nebuchadnezzar, containing the most precious and the vilest materials, heaped together without order, in strange contrast.' Antony's funeral oration is the best thing in the play, and he patriotically declares that 'the Italian *Cesare* of the Abate Antonio Conti possesses far greater merits,' though it is, of course, inferior to Voltaire's play. In his *Ragionamento sopra il Diletto della Tragedia* he protests against the horrors of sight being added to those inherent in the action itself 'as in Shakespeare's *Andronicus, Hamlet* and *Henry VI*, and the majority of English tragedies.' In his opinion Philoctetes is a sight more suited for a hospital than a tragedy. A refined taste should steer a middle course between the narrative of the Greek and the action of the English stage.

A fondness for horrors is the charge most consistently brought against our dramatists, after their neglect of the unities, till well into the nineteenth century. Riccoboni we have already mentioned. Giambattista Roberti repeats it more than once. He calls Shakespeare 'bloody' in a letter of 3 May, 1775, while in his *Dell' Amor verso la Patria*,[1] he says that you must be able to do something more than 'handle corpses like Shakespeare' if you want to move your audience. Similarly in *La Commedia*[2] we read that

[1] *Opere*, Vol. VIII. p. 89.   [2] *Opere*, Vol. IX. p. 205.

Sovra del Britanno palco
Troppo imperversa la man tinta e lorda
Di caldo sangue la crudel Tragedia.

As late as 1813 Raimondo Grimaldi, in his *Saggio
aella Tragedia*, laments the applause given to tragedies
which inspire nothing but a taste for blood and treachery.
Even Voltaire is among the guilty, but the chief offenders
are Shakespeare and all the English tragic poets, with
the exception of the truly noble 'Adisson'.

Agostino Paradisi, Algarotti's friend, 'curious in the
highest degree to make the acquaintance of that much
decried poet', has finished *Julius Cæsar* and is reading
Macbeth, he tells Algarotti in a letter (30 January,
1760). 'What can I say about such an author? There
are beauties, I see, but the defects are too great and
too numerous. Yet I can imagine that an Englishman
will find pretty things there which it is not given to
those uninitiated into the mysteries of the language to
discover.'[1] So Stefano Arteaga, in the Preface to his
Rivoluzioni del Teatro Musicale (1785), says that a man
of taste admires, but does not imitate Shakespeare,
Calderon and Lope de Vega, and prefers Molière to
the comedy-writers of all ages.

According to Francesco Milizia, in his *Trattato completo,
formale e materiale del Teatro* (1773), p. 24, Shakespeare
handled tragedy with astonishing greatness and insufferable defects. 'Johnson took many irregularities from it ;
Addison gave it all correctness.' Chinese plays, he says
elsewhere, are without the three unities and defective in

---

[1] Algarotti, *Opere*, Vol. XIII. p. 294.

the essential rules, 'like the monstrous farces of Shakespeare and Lope de Vega, which are called tragedies.'
And we may here mention the wish expressed by the
author of *Osservazioni fatte da un Viaggiatore in alcuni
Paesi d'Europa* (1787), p. 40, that Shakespeare's works
had been scattered to the winds like his ashes.

Milizia's comparison was not allowed to drop, however. Pietro Napoli-Signorelli's *Storia Critica de' Teatri
Antichi e Moderni* (1777) informs us that Shakespeare
'had no better knowledge of the rules of probability
than the Chinese. Like them he compressed the events
of thirty years into a performance of a few hours and
was inferior to Thespis himself in not separating tragedy
from comedy. Yet he was a genius full of an enthusiasm
which raises him at times almost to the level of Euripides
and his countrymen are right in affirming that he abounds
in faults innumerable and beauties inimitable. . . . He
was ignorant of art and drew vigorously from Nature.
What a matchless poet might be produced by the study
of them both!' (pp. 246–7). One thinks of Pope :—

> In all debates, where critics bear a part,
> Not one but nods, and talks of Jonson's art,
> And Shakespeare's nature.

But on page 388 we read that the enthusiasm for
liberty, the pride and melancholy of Britain, the fire of
passion and of the language, and the tendency to suicide,
which so interested visitors to our shores at this time,
'have a wonderful effect upon English tragedy and
give it such life and vigour that the French appears

to languish like a delicate rose-colour beside a strong purple in comparison.' This is indeed a concession. Whatever knowledge of Shakespeare the author may have possessed, the biographical details he supplies (pp. 246–7) are very inaccurate.

In his *Elementi di Poesia Drammatica* (1801, Anno X) Napoli-Signorelli considers it a fault for 'servants, soldiers, women and shepherds to express themselves with mythological, historical and learned pedantry as we see them doing in Shakespear,' who is also blamed for so utterly improbably mixing verse with prose (pp. 19–20). But, like Voltaire, he quotes the fact that 'the actor-author Shakespear and the celebrated actress Ofields' have honoured monuments at Westminster as proof of the praiseworthy importance attached to the theatre in England (p. 39). According to Vincenzo Marenco in *Lo Spirito del Patriotismo riguardo alle Scienze* (1783), p. 84, Shakespeare may be ranked with Sophocles and Corneille for fire and enthusiasm, 'though he is inferior to them in elegance of language and in the conduct of his dramas, which ought to be called tragi-comedies rather than tragedies.'

Aurelio Bertòla is more interesting. He first introduced German literature into Italy, and in his *Idea della Bella Letteratura* (1784), he sighs as he thinks of the glory Goethe might win for himself and the German theatre 'if he would one day realise that irregularity can only deceive for a short time; that Shakespeare, idolised by his own nation, has only a few scenes for the rest of Europe, and that a man runs great risk of

losing sight of nature if he loses sight of the divine
models of the Greeks, to which alone Racine and
Maffei owe the merit of being admired by all nations and
all ages.' Bertòla, therefore, places Maffei above Shakespeare, just as Cesarotti had placed Conti. Unfortunately
for his criticism, which is, of course, borrowed from
Voltaire, Schröder, the famous German actor, had already
begun his successful performances of Shakespeare in
Hamburg. Another patriotic critic in the *Nuovo Giornale
Letterario d'Italia* (Venice, 1789), p. 20, prefers *Antonio
e Cleopatra* by Antonio Marescalchi, Senator of Bologna,
to Shakespeare's play. Shakespeare is a mere 'copista
di Plutarco', with a fondness for buffoonery which
allows him to put into the Queen of Egypt's mouth
the expression, 'Let us to billiards'. 'Could anyone
be so stupid as to dare to offer us as a model to be
imitated a tragedy in which the heroine asks to play at
billiards?' One remembers that a tragedy of Voltaire's
failed because he allowed a queen to drink a poisoned
cup upon the stage. If it was not patriotism, it was
doubtless a translator's prejudice which allowed Luigi
Richeri to rank Shakespeare below Edward Young in
the Introduction to his version of the latter's *Revenge*
in 1790.

But perhaps the best proof of Voltaire's power of
doing mischief is to be found in Giovanni Andres's
Dell' Origine, Progressi e Stato Attuale d'Ogni Letteratura.
Andres was a Spanish Jesuit, but a beautiful edition of
his work was issued by the Royal Press of Parma in
1785. In writing of Addison's *Cato* he says that he

feels some diffidence in discussing the style of a work written in a foreign language 'with which I have not sufficient acquaintance to be able to form an exact opinion'. He had read Warton's *History of English Poetry* and knows something of our early playwrights, yet this is how he speaks of Shakespeare (Vol. II. p. 343): 'Shakespeare is the idol of the English,' and even some Frenchmen (doubtless Le Tourneur and his friends) have been bitten with the craze. 'But whatever his enthusiastic admirers may say, I cannot find these much-vaunted beauties in his works; nor, if they really existed, do I think it wise or worth the trouble to look for them in the midst of so much filth. . . . Read with an unbiased mind all the passages marked as excellent by Pope; read even the scene in *Antonio* so highly praised by Sherlok [*sic*], and then say frankly whether the few, the very few expressive, pathetic and eloquent passages are enough to set against the frequent, nay, almost continuous stupidity and folly which deface them. . . . But even if we allow some merit to the most famous passages, how can anyone have the courage to read a whole play?' This question throws light upon Andres's acquaintance with the subject. 'Some parts of *Hamlet, Cæsar, Othello, Macbeth* and his other tragedies may be as excellent and divine as you like; but who, on this account, can endure to see a mouse, a wall, a lion, moonlight appear and speak and act and take part in the dialogue, to listen to coarse, vulgar talk, and jokes of shoemakers, tailors, gravediggers and the lowest of the people; to hear trivial jests, indecent

words and common scurrility from the lips of princes
and people of the highest respectability; and in fact be
obliged to read endless fantastic things and intoler-
able extravagances? Anyone desiring to learn what
Shakespeare's tragedies are really like must not go to
Voltaire's *Mort de César*, nor to *Hamlet* and *King Lear*
and other tragedies of Ducis, nor to the translations of
La Place and Le Tourneur. He must read them in
the original, or at least in Voltaire's absolutely literal
and faithful rendering of *Julius Cæsar* in his commentary
on Corneille, and in the analysis of *Hamlet* he made
under the name of Carre.' Elsewhere he says that
Shakespeare and Vondel have been called the English
and the Dutch Corneille, but Vondel is inferior even
to Shakespeare. The *Nuovo Giornale dei Letterati d'Italia*
(Vol. XXXIV. p. 385), devotes three articles to Andres's
work, observing that he discusses Shakespeare at length
and is sparing of praise to 'Addisson's' *Cato*. Andres
was a man of considerable ability and better equipped
for passing an opinion on Shakespeare than the majority
of critics of his day. Yet he can urge his readers in all
seriousness to form their opinions on Shakespeare from
Voltaire's deliberate travesties. Is it surprising in the
circumstances that Voltaire could trade so long and so
successfully upon the ignorance of his own countrymen?

III

ANGLOMANIA AND MORE FAVOURABLE JUDGMENTS

But there is another side to the picture. If Voltaire to
a great extent stereotyped the Shakespeare criticism of
the day, his visit to England was a no less important
factor in the growth of the Anglomania which invaded
France and spread thence through the whole of Europe
during the latter half of the eighteenth century. English
influence was, of course, inferior to that of France in
Italy, but it acted as a supplement and a corrective to
the prevailing Gallomania. The whole question has
been admirably dealt with in Arturo Graf's *L'Anglomania
e l'Influsso Inglese in Italia nel Secolo XVIII*. Not only
were Italian visitors to England far more frequent, but
the popularity of Italian opera in London and the conse-
quent demand for Italian masters among the upper classes
had drawn a number of literary adventurers to London,
who picked up a precarious living by teaching modern
languages and writing libretti for the opera. Their
abilities were well above the average and they did something to promote an interest in things English among
their countrymen at home.

Consequently, instead of being the 'ultima Thule',
England was rapidly becoming the promised land. The
English constitution, English life and manners, science
and philosophy, legislation and political economy were

eagerly studied, and advocates of trade, as opposed to agriculture, like the brothers Pietro and Alessandro Verri in Milan, pointed triumphantly to England's prosperity. Italians, indeed, have little affection for the lower classes in England who called them 'French dogs', a name applied contemptuously to all foreigners, even Turks with long beards. They are horrified at the freedom they enjoy. According to Alessandro Verri the vulgar Englishman's idea of liberty is to be able to say and write just what he thinks about everyone from God Almighty to a street porter. Yet Verri receives little sympathy from his brother. On being told that an Englishman, after nearly knocking an Italian down in the Park, had coolly replied that he must learn to give way to an Englishman, Count Pietro writes : 'It is natural to our *amour propre* to regret our inferiority as a nation, but reason is on the side of the English. They are markedly superior to the rest of the Continent of Europe and are right to treat foreigners as slaves.' Could Anglomania go further than this ? And London made every other place seem 'small and mean' even to Alessandro Verri after his return home.

But with the upper classes it is different. It is true that they are not hospitable to foreigners and are unwilling to welcome them to their homes, and the English custom of heavy drinking after dinner is universally condemned ; but De Gamerra has summed up the general feeling in his comedy, *Il Generoso Inglese* (1779), iii. 8. Our nobility are 'the best informed, the most enlightened, the wisest and the bravest in Europe.' Baretti saw our faults as clearly as anyone, yet he places us 'quite at the head of mankind' and likes to describe himself as 'a kind of demi-Englishman', while Algarotti considers that in no nation will you find so close a resemblance to ancient Rome—surely the highest compliment an eighteenth-century Italian could pay us. Indeed, we soon find the English 'Milordo' crystallized as a popular character who puts everything right in the plays of the day. 'Few words and many sequins' is the verdict on Milord Stunkle in Albergati's *Ciarlator Maldicente*, and these are his usual characteristics. Graf considers this enthusiasm for a character and manners so utterly unlike their own as one of the most curious phenomena in the history of Italian civilization.

But the enthusiasm for our men was as nothing compared with that for our women. They won all Italian hearts from the days of Giordano Bruno onwards, though Bruno in the sixteenth century, like Ugo Foscolo in the nineteenth, heaves a little sigh over their hearts of adamant. Baretti, who was intimate with many of the most charming of them—the Hornecks and the Burneys, for instance—may be supposed to speak with the greatest authority, and he is second to none in the chorus of praise. Alessandro Verri, fresh from Paris, writes from London that he had never before realized the power of beauty. 'The excellent meat they eat, the fact that the sun is not oppressively hot and is often hidden by fog, and the temperate climate all combine to give a freshness to their complexions and a round-ness and softness to their cheeks that makes them quite irresistible. Every woman's face here means something ; they are all animated.' Moreover, English cutlery, watches, magnifying glasses, leather, metal, salt fish, furniture, horses and carriages, even cider, punch, beer and tea had their devotees.

Though English literature did not play a leading part in the craze, it was by no means neglected. At this time it was in close touch with the main current on the continent, where French dictatorship was supreme, and the high opinion in which English literature, to say nothing of English philosophy, was held in Paris rapidly attracted attention in Italy. 'To translate something from the English, especially poetry, was almost obligatory for anyone laying claim to the title of man of letters in our country,' says Graf, 'and it would be easy to organise a procession, beginning with Conti and Rolli and ending with Foscolo.' According to Denina,[1] the influence exercised by England upon Italian literature 'is much more marked than in Spain and hardly less than in France'.

But apart from Milton, who was duly appreciated from the first, it was the typical writers of the day who became popular in Italy, as in France. 'Adisson's' *Cato*, backed by Voltaire's approval, was adopted as eagerly as the great man's spelling of the name. The French translation of the *Spectator* (Amsterdam, 1746) soon found a ready audience. Verri imitated it in his *Caffè*, and Gaspare Gozzi in the *Osservatore*. Baretti, who modelled his *Frusta Letteraria* upon it, told Johnson

[1] *Discorso sulle Vicende della Letteratura*, II. 98.

D

that his admiration for the *Spectator* was the principal
reason for his wishing to come to England. Swift, too,
was read and admired, but Pope was by far the most
popular of our writers. Maffei calls Pope the English
Voltaire in a letter to Voltaire himself, and his influence
was not very much less.

But literature of this kind did little to prepare the
way for Shakespeare. It served rather to reinforce the
prevailing prejudice against him. Far more important
for our purposes was the vogue enjoyed by the melancholy grave poetry, which originated in England and
reached the peninsula, as usual, through France. Gray's
Elegy was a special favourite and was frequently translated. But it was to Young that the writers of these
melancholy *Younghiana*, as Carducci calls them, looked
up as their leader. Baretti saw their true value when he
said that 'before a century is passed, the worms, which
often do their work very slowly, will have devoured
all the blank verse of Trapp and Young'. Yet
Mrs. Piozzi writes from Padua that 'Gray and Young
are the favourite writers among us so far as I have yet
heard them talked over upon the continent'.[1] But an
even more noteworthy harbinger of romanticism was
Macpherson's *Ossian*. Cesarotti's admirable sonorous
blank verse rendering (1763) was carrying all before it
by the end of the century. The *Nuovo Giornale dei
Letterati* considers Ossian 'a genius of the same order
as Homer, Dante, Milton,' and admirers even ranked
him above Homer. Like the Great Napoleon, Monti,

[1] *Observations and Reflections made in the course of a journey*, &c., p. 225.

Foscolo and most of the young men of the rising generation fell under the spell. Angelo Mazza even tells us of a barber in Parma who was an enthusiast.

When these pre-Romantics were making their way in Italy, it is not surprising to find that, though Voltaire's opinion upon Shakespeare still dominates the field, there are more favourable judgments to set against it. Goldoni has a good deal to say about Shakespeare. There were a number of English residents in Venice, and during the Carnival English visitors swarmed there and were very popular, owing to their wealth. Anglomania flourished. By 1754 the *Spectator* was in everybody's hands, Goldoni tells us in the Preface to his *Filosofo Inglese*, which was produced there on 4 January of that year. Even the ladies, who did not read much in those days, caught the fashion and turned philosophers, and probably began to ask who Shakespeare was. Goldoni, as usual, turned the craze to account in this play, where he tells us that 'Sachespar' 'fu gran poeta e tragico politico'. To the same year belongs the *Malcontenti*, in which he satirizes his rival Chiari as Grisologo, a foolish imitator of 'Sachespir', as it is here spelt. It was first played at Verona in the summer of 1755, but was prohibited in Venice owing to the attacks on Chiari, and was never performed there. Grisologo writes both tragedy and comedy and is asked whether he has taken the good or the bad from Sachespir. His play is called the *Life of Cromwell, Protector of England*. 'The Life of Cromwell? The life of a man in a single comedy,' ask Grisologo's friends. 'Yes, sir,' answers

Grisologo. 'Sachespir, a celebrated English author, has written the *Life and Death of Richard III.*' When the style is criticized as too elevated for a comedy, Grisologo bids his critic read Sachespir. 'Read his *Merry Wives* or *Women of Windsor.* Read his *Sogno di Una Notte.*'

Goldoni found a number of English plays in the library of Professor Lanzio at Pavia, with whom he stayed before entering the college there ; but as he knew no English Shakespeare would have been a sealed book to him, in the improbable case of his being among them. But it is quite likely that Goldoni had learned something about Shakespeare from John Murray, the English Resident in Venice, to whom he dedicated the play two years later. Indeed, he tells Murray in the dedication that, though ignorant of English, he has endeavoured to profit by translations of the best works. One is reminded of Metastasio's letter to Calzabigi. All the political and moral worth to be found in his writings, he proceeds, is the result of careful imitation of English originals.

'Your famous Shakespeare [spelt correctly this time] —worthy of respect among foreign nations, no less than in British theatres—has completely harmonised in himself the gifts of comedy and tragedy. He is at the head of the numberless English writers who have been the glory of the stage, and even to-day they prefer him to all others. In fact, his work displays such skill in developing a plot, such truth in the characters, such force in the sentiments, that he should be a model to anyone desirous of entering so arduous a profession. He has not scrupulously observed in his work those unities of time and place which cramp the imagination of a poet. In this he follows the freedom of the Spaniards, who also revolted against Aristotle's precepts. . . . For my part, I am convinced that Aristotle in his *Poetics* and his imitator, Horace, have done us more harm than good. . . . The English and the Spaniards, as I have said, freed from these cramping fetters and seriously believing that theatrical representations are only a reasonable imitation of human actions, whether tragic or comic, in accordance with the characters or the subject which the author has chosen to develop, kept themselves free to extend the action to the time necessary for the complete accomplishment of the historical facts.' So with changes of scene. The spectator's imagination must supply the gaps. 'But the rigid followers of Aristotle and Horace have the utmost difficulty in observing the unities and violate the rules of reason dictated by nature and approved by all peoples.' He has therefore shown us Grisologo imitating Shakespeare without a full knowledge of the craft of the playwright. 'Hence I have availed myself of this opportunity of proclaiming my veneration for an author so respectable and of making his name known to such as did not happen to have heard of it.'

It cannot be said that these remarks display any profound knowledge of Shakespeare, or that Goldoni treats him with much respect in the play itself, though it has been suggested with little probability that the idea of a play written in a play was actually borrowed by him from Shakespeare. The popularity of the

Spectator must have aroused curiosity about him, but Goldoni may well have learnt all he knew from talk with John Murray and other English friends upon the subject. Still, it is interesting to find Shakespeare thus early becoming the banner under which the opponents of the unities range themselves, though, as we have seen, Goldoni avoids openly violating them himself and never reprinted the dedication.

Carlo Gozzi, Goldoni's formidable rival, also avails himself of Shakespeare's name against the critics of his fantastic *Fiabe*. In *The longest letter of reply ever written, sent by Carlo Gozzi to an Italian dramatic poet of our day*, as he calls it,[1] he asks his enemies how it is that Shakespeare, by means of his dramatic works, which combine tragedy, comedy, history, magic and the fabulous, as well as vulgar coarseness and impossibilities, has had the power to stir the hearts of the spectators, to excite in them terror, horror, surprise, pity, tears, laughter ; to win for himself after his death the honour of a magnificent monument in Westminster Abbey, and a statue in the market-place of 'Stralfort', his native town, to say nothing of commentaries upon his works among foreign nations, and, lastly, to achieve immortality throughout the ages. He carefully prints the comparisons made between Shakespeare and himself by Pepoli and Baretti, though Baretti considerably modified his opinions when he came to read the *Fiabe* in print. Gozzi does, however, apologize for his presumptuousness in quoting, in his own defence, the

[1] *Opere*, Vol. XIV.

IL GIULIO
CESARE
TRAGEDIA ISTORICA
D I
GUGLIELMO
SHAKESPEARE

Tradotta dall' Inglese in Lingua Toscana

D A L   D O T T O R

DOMENICO
VALENTINI

Profeffore di Storia Ecclefiaftica
Nell' Univerfità di Siena.

IN SIENA L' ANNO · MDCCLVI.
✳✳✳✳✳✳✳✳✳✳✳✳✳✳✳✳✳✳✳✳✳✳✳✳✳✳✳✳✳✳
Nella Sramperìa di Agoſtino Bindi
Con licenza de' Superiori

immortals 'Menander, Aristophanes, Homer, Virgil, Dante, Ariosto, Tasso, Shakespeare'. But as J. Cooper Walker, who was present at the opening of the Fenice theatre in Venice in 1792, relates that 'it was not a little gratifying to an admirer of Shakespeare to see the bust of his favourite bard placed in a colonnade amongst the greatest ancient and modern dramatic poets',[1] there was nothing new in Gozzi's classification.

In the year of the publication of Goldoni's *Malcontenti*, with the dedication to Murray, there appeared the first Italian translation of a play by Shakespeare. Voltaire's imitations and criticisms had drawn attention to *Julius Cæsar*. The subject was, in any case, one likely to interest Italians. Hence *Il Giulio Cesare, Tragedia Istorica di Guglielmo Shakespeare*, translated into the Tuscan tongue by Dr. Domenico Valentini (Siena, 1756), was a wise choice. Borck's German version of the play was the only complete translation to precede it. Valentini was Professor of Ecclesiastical History in the University of Sienna, and the greater part of the lengthy Preface is taken up with a discussion of the qualifications needful for a translator. His own were not ideal. 'It is well known to everyone', he tells us, 'that owing to my natural impatience I do not understand English, but some gentlemen of that illustrious nation, who are thoroughly familiar with the Tuscan tongue, have had the kindness and the patience to explain this tragedy to me.' However, Valentini was no worse off than Ducis, who was obliged to go to La Place for the knowledge of Shakespeare upon which his modernizations are based.

[1] *Historical Memoirs of Italian Tragedy*, p. 291.

M. Paul Hazard[1] draws attention to the patriotic
endeavours of English residents to awaken interest in
English literature in Italy. They did much to supplement
the efforts of Italians who had travelled in England.
Charles Sackville first introduced Cesarotti to Ossian,
and helped him in his translation, while Lord Bute not
only paid the expenses of the first edition, but made
the author a present of the proceeds of the sales. This
was in Venice, where the English colony was large
and where there was a great trade in translations of
all kinds. Salvini's version of *Cato* was begun at the
suggestion of the English residents at Leghorn, who
were at least as numerous as those in Venice. It is also
obvious that Murray endeavoured to interest Goldoni
in Shakespeare. An Italian professor at Padua told
Mrs. Piozzi that no Englishman could sit for three
hours together without talking of Shakespeare.[2]

Even Englishmen of humble station helped in the
good work. Angela Veronese was a minor poetess of
some distinction in the Veneto in her day, under her
Arcadian name of Aglaja Anassillide. Her father was
a gardener, and in the interesting and amusing autobiography prefixed to her poems she tells how Count
Alvise Zenobio, at that time the patron of her family,
had spent several years in England, fascinated by the
peculiarities of our nation. 'On returning to his native
land he brought with him two English servants, the
one a devotee of the bottle, the other of books.' The

[1] *Les Littératures du Nord et l'Esprit Latin en Italie*, in *Studien zur vergleichenden
Literaturgeschichte*, **IX**. 3.   [2] *Observations and Reflections*, p. 225.

lady considers the former the wiser of the two, since the bottle relieved his native gloom, whereas the other only increased it by his reading. However, he 'explained to my father in bad Italian Shakespeare's highly esteemed works, my father repeated the accounts to his friend the chaplain and I, who was always present, learnt them by heart even better than he did. The result was that my head was stuffed with poisoned kings, sleep-walking queens, witches and tender-hearted murderers.' These early lessons have left no trace upon the work of the fair poetess, which is altogether conventional, but this was not the fault of the patriotic groom.[1]

And now we find Valentini's English friends actively assisting him in his translation of *Julius Cæsar* in Sienna. On the whole they are to be congratulated on their performance. This prose rendering is quite undistinguished, but it is pretty accurate. Considerable pains have been taken to reproduce the puns in the first scene, for instance, which are omitted altogether by La Place. In the effort to bring out Shakespeare's meaning clearly the Italian is often much longer than the original, as, for instance, at the end of Brutus's soliloquy at the beginning of Act ii, Scene i. But as a rule the text is closely adhered to. In the Preface Valentini follows Voltaire and the early English commentators, giving it as his opinion that any attempt to confine an imagination such as Shakespeare's within the rules would have killed it. Shakespeare's faults are due to the time at which he lived and are compensated by 'thoughts so noble, so

[1] Aglaja Anassillide, *Poesie Scelte*, pp. 24–5.

luminous, painted in colours so glorious, so vivid that every sensible and unprejudiced reader will regard them as venial.' If he mingled the sublime with the vulgar, it is because he was forced to do so by his subject. He was obliged to bring plebeians on the stage, and their characters, though vulgar, are natural throughout the play. His subject, too, made changes of scene necessary.

These criticisms have obviously been contributed by his English friends. They resemble the apologetic tone which even Shakespeare's English admirers felt bound to adopt in defending him in the prevailing state of opinion. Hume, Chesterfield and Goldsmith were hostile, and Charles James Fox thought that Shakespeare's fame would have stood higher if he had not written *Hamlet*, probably on account of the gravediggers, whom Garrick omitted altogether. Hugh Blair's once famous *Lectures on Rhetoric and Belles Lettres* (1783) held a position of its own among works of criticism. Soave's translation of it remained a text-book in use in Italian schools till the middle of last century. Corniani quotes Blair frequently and always with respect. Yet Shakespeare, he tells us, 'is a genius shooting wild, deficient in just taste and altogether unassisted by nature and art. . . . There is hardly any one of his plays which can be called altogether a good one and which can be read with uninterrupted pleasure from beginning to end.' It is true that he elsewhere realizes that Shakespeare's beauties far outweigh his faults, but is it surprising that Shakespeare was long in coming into his own in a country where this was probably the best known English judgment upon him? Certainly no Italian of Valentini's attainments could have written of him as he writes of him in his Preface at this time. From the same source he doubless derived the few biographical facts he gives, quoting Theobald as his authority.

Valentini's translation did not meet with an encouraging reception. Zaccaria wrote in the *Annali Letterari d'Italia*, Vol. I. Pt. I. pp. 42–3, that 'the word historical explains everything' and calls it, probably remembering Cesarotti, 'a slice of exaggerated history'. The number of the characters and the violation of the unities are bad enough, but what is to be said when the savage actually has Cæsar murdered *coram populo*?

But events were moving. We read of Giambattista Biffi, a friend of the Verris and of Beccaria, including extracts from Shakespeare, as well as from Addison, Swift, Hume, Pope and Dryden in a manuscript note-book about 1760.[1] And Biccherai asks :[2] 'Who would not prefer the fate of his [Shakespeare's] tragedies to that of Gravina's or Conti's? The violation of a law makes a play to some extent improbable, shocking, extraordinary—faults far less serious than coldness or dulness.' It is possible that this is a reminiscence of the *Spectator* (No. 592) : 'Who would not rather read one of his plays, where there is not a single rule of the stage observed, than any production of a modern critick, where there is not one of them violated?' But the judgment is none the less noteworthy.

---

[1] Graf, *Anglomania*, p. 236.
[2] *Tragedie e Considerazioni sul Teatro Italiano* (1767).

Ranieri dei Calzabigi also shows an appreciation of Shakespeare unusual at this time in his well-known letter to Alfieri on his tragedies (1783): 'The English, if we except not whole tragedies, which are far more defective than ours, but a few sublime passages from the celebrated Shakspeare, are as poorly off as we are. . . . This illustrious nation, which affects a manner and system of thought different from all others, a nation free and proud, has been eager to prove its independence, even in tragedy. As with its government, it has adopted a special tragic constitution of its own for its theatre. It is satisfied with it, nay, proud of it, in spite of the outcries of all the others. For the famous Shakspeare, author of this new constitution, the unities are fetters fitted for slaves. . . . He produced monstrosities, but they were original. . . . In his dramas you have a harrowing massacre in one scene, while you laugh in the next. He did not care to embellish nature, but showed her, as she was in his day, cruel, rough, savage. Savage too, truth to tell, were the characters he brought upon the stage and perhaps also the audience present at these entertainments of his. He introduced spectres and ghosts happily and with great success, and in my opinion with great wisdom : they are, whatever one may say, the most effective means of arousing terror and were especially suited to the cruel and superstitious minds of his contemporaries. To such an audience mere death meant nothing. Horror must be piled on horror. He mixed prose with verse and the trivial with the sublime, but with this peculiarity, that his trivial is

that of the common herd, his sublime that of Longinus.'
In Calzabigi's opinion French tragedy is unquestionably
the best in existence, in spite of its faults.

Later on he tells us that Shakespeare 'has a manner
extravagant, rough, savage, but he draws to the life,
reproduces the characters of his creations to the life.'
It is true that Calzabigi goes on to say that in fire and
vigour Alfieri is more like Shakespeare than anyone
else, though, of course, the refined taste of the age in
which he lived raised him above Shakespeare.   But
compliments of this kind were mere good manners
when a literary man was writing to a brother of the
craft about his work ; and some allowance must be
made for his delight at the appearance of a great tragic
poet in Italy at last. However, he goes on to give
good blank verse renderings of two passages from
Richard III, the only play translated in its entirety by
La Place, 'Give me another horse' (v. 4), and 'Send
to her by the hand that slew her brothers' (iv. 4), and
also of a part of Romeo's last speech, 'O my love, my
wife !' (v. 3).

In his *Saggio sulla Musica Imitativa Teatrale* (1781),[1]
Matteo Borsa is speaking of the expression of violent
passions. 'So that beautiful passage of Shakespeare in
his *Macbeth* who, [*sic*] on hearing from a friend the
fatal news of the murder of his wife and children by
the sword of the enemy, is seized with a profound, over-
mastering melancholy : and on hearing himself urged
by the same friend to the destruction, the slaughter of

[1] *Opuscoli scelti sulle Scienze e sulle Arti*, Vol. IV. p. 206.

his enemy, to revenge, answers shortly : "He has no children." What music, what song, what modulation of notes will ever achieve this unapproachable answer ?' Here at least is sympathetic criticism. But the passage was rapidly becoming a commonplace. Ducis transferred it to his version of *Romeo and Juliet*, and Borsa's mistake in assigning the remark to Macbeth raises a doubt as to whether he had read the play at all. Yet Carlo Marenco could imitate Macduff's answer in the Doge's reply to Donati's expressions of sympathy, 'E non t'è figlio', in his *Famiglia Foscari* (i. 3), which was not published till 1835.

But we are at last beginning to find genuine Italian admirers of Shakespeare, who are thoroughly familiar with his work. Chief among these was Johnson's friend, Giuseppe Baretti (1719–89), who came to England in 1751. He studied our literature eagerly from the first, and we may feel sure that Johnson early introduced him to Shakespeare. 'Should anybody weigh, for instance, Shakespeare in the Aristotelian scales,' he says in the *Italian Library* (1757), 'he would find him much defective ; yet was not Shakespeare at least as great a tragic as any Grecian ? . . . Consult your heart rather than Aristotle when you read.' On his returning to Italy to edit the *Frusta Letteraria* (1763–5), the little paper modelled on the *Spectator*, or rather on the *Rambler*, which made an epoch in criticism there, Johnson sent him his Shakespeare 'that you may explain his works to the ladies of Italy, and tell them the story of the editor, among the other strange narratives with which your long residence in this unknown region has supplied you.' Baretti had already attacked the unities in the second Preface to his translation of Corneille (1747–8), pointing out that Metastasio gave pleasure whether read, listened to or sung, though 'he did not pay too much attention to Father Aristotle's precepts,' whereas Conti and Maffei, for all their correctness, were far more read than played. In the *Frusta*, however, he was too busy lashing the feeble literature of the day to give more than passing references to Shakespeare. It is true that in No. 6 he says that Orlando's madness moves him more profoundly than that of the Greek Philoctetes or the English King Lear, but in No. 8 he tells Denina that Shakespeare is a poet 'who, both in tragedy and comedy, is by himself a match for all the Corneilles, all the Racines and all the Molières of Gaul.' Like Ariosto he is one of those 'transcendent poets, "whose genius soars beyond the reach of art."' The violence of the *Frusta* drew forth an equally violent reply from Appiano Bonafede, the *Bue Pedagogo* (1765), in which he takes Baretti to task for praising Shakespeare because he could always draw crowds to the theatre, when he had held Goldoni up to scorn on account of this very popularity. He also quotes an English writer's strictures on Shakespeare for his love of puns, and retails a number of Voltaire's criticisms on '*Hamelet*' as a proof of the absurdity of Baretti's enthusiasm. In the fifth of his discourses in reply to the *Bue Pedagogo* Baretti refuses altogether to discuss the rubbish Bonafede talks about Shakespeare on the word of Voltaire. Why does he meddle with the English language and the tragedy of *Hamlet* and Shakespeare's other works, when he knows nothing about them?

With Voltaire Baretti had long had a special quarrel owing to his treatment of Dante and Ariosto. Hence, when Voltaire sent his famous letter to the French Academy in 1776, attacking Shakespeare, after the appearance of the first two volumes of Le Tourneur's translation, Baretti determined to reply. The *Discours sur Shakespeare et sur Monsieur de Voltaire*, written in French, appeared in London in 1778. Like Mrs. Montagu, he asserted that Voltaire did not know English. His translations of Shakespeare are often inaccurate, or so literal as to make the English poet seem ridiculous. Are these mistakes due to ignorance or to malice? Perhaps he is afraid that Le Tourneur's translation will show up his blunders. If so, he can reassure himself. Poetry is rarely translatable and such translations are little read. Moreover, Shakespeare's poetry could not be translated with even moderate success into a Latin tongue, because its beauties are altogether different from those of a language derived from Latin. Shakespeare knew neither Latin nor Greek, nor any other language, but he possessed a profound knowledge of human nature. At the age of thirty-two he had formed a style which is at times vulgar and affected, but more often closely-knit, forcible and passionate, producing a poetry that carries one off one's feet when he wishes to do so. French is too exact to reproduce his rough genius. Voltaire's attempts to translate him into blank verse, a metre utterly contrary to the spirit of the French language, can only be meant to make him appear ridiculous. He is unrecognizable in Alexandrines, which Baretti admirably likens to 'a procession of monks, marching two and two, with solemn measured tread along a straight road,' while in prose he is like a hash without salt. In any case, to try to give Shakespeare in samples is as aburd as to give a brick as a sample of a house—a comparison which Baretti borrowed from Johnson's Preface. To understand him you must spend years in England studying the language. Then you must study Shakespeare's English and see him acted, though, since Garrick's retirement, you will no longer be able to see his greatest interpreter. 'If you stay quietly at home and rely on Sieur Le Tourneur, Hélas! But if you put your trust in M. de Voltaire, Holà!'[1]

In discussing the unities Baretti uses the arguments first systematically tabulated by Johnson, but there is nothing apologetic in his tone. He will not allow Aristotle any authority whatever, and is as uncompromising in his onslaught as a leader of the romantic movement. Personal observation has taught him that *Hamlet* and *Macbeth* are far more popular in London than *Bajazet* or *Polyeucte* in Paris. The greater variety of character and action in Shakespeare make this quite

[1] A parody on Boileau's epigram on Corneille's failures :—

> Après l'Agésilas,
>   Hélas!
> Après l'Attila,
>   Holà!

intelligible. He even declares that a time will come
when the artificialities of the French stage will no
longer be endured, and the works of Corneille and his
imitators will be banished from the theatre to the
library. Voltaire calls *Cato* the only reasonable English
tragedy. But the English possess a number of tragedies
of this kind, as well as translations from the French,
though they are far less popular than Shakespeare. In
fact, they are rich in both styles. Voltaire says that
there are more than thirty thousand good judges of
the drama in Paris. But there are more people qualified
to criticize Greek authors in this island than perhaps
in all the rest of Europe, since there are more gentlemen able to read Sophocles and Euripides in the original.
Not that he wishes to proscribe the French methods.
He would give a finger to be able to write a tragedy
as good as *Cinna*. 'I say this in all seriousness. But
must I say it? I would give two for the power of
creating a character as good as Caliban in the *Tempest*.'
In fact, like the Romantics, Baretti was fighting for
liberty. He had no objection to the classical school in
itself, but he insisted that this was not the only way
to write tragedy. Shakespeare had as good a right to
serious consideration as Sophocles or Racine.

Voltaire should have noted Shakespeare's merits, not
his defects; 'his marvellous gift for creating characters
as real as they are extraordinary', of which even his
poorest plays furnish instances. 'Among Shakespeare's
most striking characters, I cannot express enough admiration for Caliban, whom I have mentioned above. It

requires a highly poetic imagination to invent such a man and yet to make him altogether probable, in spite of the impossibility of his existing.' And he proceeds to describe him. 'This is the creature whom Shakespeare has endowed with reason and love. But what love! What reason! Neither more nor less than a monster born of an evil spirit and one of the most evil of witches would possess. His ideas are as novel as his sentiments. Yet they are none the less founded upon the greatest truths of Nature. It would require an extraordinarily fine painter to add anything to the picture.' Baretti is doubtless indebted for the germ of these remarks to the *Spectator* (Nos. 279 and 419), where Addison discusses Caliban and Shakespeare's fairies and other supernatural beings. But they have developed considerably in his hands.

'Look at Shylock in the play called the *Merchant of Venice*. . . . What shall I say of Falstaff, the inimitable Falstaff?' In fact, Baretti could not even give slight sketches of Shakespeare's great creations. 'Farceur,' says Voltaire. 'Oh, blasphème poétique,' answers Baretti. It is worth learning English merely to read him. 'To compare Voltaire's characters with Shakespeare's is like comparing pretty ivory figures with Michelangelo's Moses or David.'

Voltaire simply makes the Ghost in *Hamlet* ridiculous by transferring it to *Sémiramis*. 'He treats Shakespeare as "histrion barbare", and "Gille de village", but what kind of a Gille or Histrion is he when he enters the arena to measure his strength with such a giant?'

Imagine the absurdity of the Ghost of Ninus appearing from a tomb in a room which has been transformed into a splendid temple for the occasion, in order to save the face of the unities, before a number of courtiers in broad daylight! Even Voltaire finds Shakespeare's Ghost far more terrible than that of Darius in the *Persæ*, because it comes to demand vengeance, not to prophesy victory. It is interesting to find Baretti adopting the same line of argument as Lessing in his *Hamburgische Dramaturgie* (1776), x–xii. As Baretti did not know German, and the French translation did not appear till 1785, he cannot possibly have been acquainted with Lessing's work. Yet his argument is virtually the same, except that Lessing sees that Shakespeare's Ghost acts upon the audience through its effect upon Hamlet, an effect which could not possibly be produced by Ninus's Ghost through the crowd of courtiers in broad daylight.[1]

Baretti possessed neither the sweet reasonableness of an Addison, nor the solid ratiocination of the great Doctor. His critical work was generally written at white heat. His fiery, impatient temperament made it difficult for him to arrange his matter systematically, and the *Discours*, especially, was hurriedly put together before the excitement over Voltaire's letter had had time to evaporate. There is something volcanic in the way in which he throws out his ideas, leaving them to cool and take shape just where they happen to fall. Moreover, he devotes almost as much space to vitu-

[1] Morandi, *Voltaire contro Shakespeare*, &c., p. 88.

perating Voltaire as to defending Shakespeare. Yet the
Discours is full of energy and enthusiasm, and is inspired
by the absolute conviction of the truth of what he is
saying that characterizes the author. Professor Nichol
Smith has, indeed, shown that during the eighteenth
century Shakespeare received far more honour in his
own country than has generally been realized; but
for all their admiration the early editors were never
altogether comfortable about Aristotle and his precious
unities. They had an uneasy suspicion that Shakspeare
ought to have know and observed them, and felt bound
to apologize for him in consequence. Johnson was the
first to declare definitely that 'the unities of time and
place are not essential to a just drama', and he defended
his opinion in some delightfully characteristic sentences.

'Delusion, if delusion be admitted, has no certain
limitation; if the spectator can be once persuaded that
his old acquaintance are Alexander and Cæsar, that
a room illuminated with candles is the plain of Pharsalia,
or the bank of Granicus, he is in a state of elevation
above the reach of reason, or of truth, and from the
heights of empyrean poetry may despise the circum-
scriptions of terrestrial nature. There is no reason why
a mind thus wandering in ecstasy should count the
clock, or why an hour should not be a century in that
calenture of the brains that can make the stage a field.'

But Johnson delivered his opinion with the modesty
of tone becoming to a pioneer, whereas Baretti was
hampered by no such considerations and, as usual,
proclaimed his doctrines as though they were part of the

immutable laws of the universe. Indeed, his *Discours* is
the most forcible statement of the case before Schlegel's
famous lectures, and this alone would make it noteworthy. He himself considered it the best thing he
had yet done,[1] and wrote to his brother Filippo that it
would greatly increase his reputation in Europe and
his popularity in England.[2] More than one modern
critic has been inclined to endorse his own judgment.
But as usual he was over-sanguine. The French
copies 'were emasculated by a clumsy Royal Censor
(G. B. Suard), a thorough Voltairian, who made Durand,
the bookseller, reprint a number of pages before allow-
ing it to appear'. In Italy Voltaire's influence was too
overpowering, and the interest in the subject too slight,
for it to attract much notice. In Paris La Harpe talked
of 'a sort of lunatic called Baretti' and his 'pamphlet
written in a style to make one die of laughing'.[3] The
Discours is not well arranged, as we have seen, and the
French is far from perfect, as Baretti knew, and his
enemies soon found out, to his cost. In his own copy,
now in the Barton Collection of the Boston Public
Library in America, it has been carefully corrected.

Baretti tells us that George III read it and liked it,
but from what we know of His Majesty's views on
Shakespeare, and Baretti's own accuracy, we may perhaps be allowed to doubt the statement. Though he
distributed a number of copies among his friends in
England it appears to have fallen quite flat. Hannah

[1] Letter to G. M. Bicetti, 3 May, 1777.   [2] 8 May, 1777.
[3] *Correspondence Adressée au Grand Duc*, II. 179.

More wrote before having read it that it was slippery ground—'an Italian author to write about our divine English dramatist and that in the French language'. The scurrilous Kenrick, who abused Baretti as systematically as he did Johnson and Garrick, calls it 'an impertinent effusion of a self-conceited foreigner, who would be thought to know everything and hardly knows anything'.[1] This is the only English criticism, if such it may be called, that it appears to have elicited. Mrs. Montagu's affected and much inferior *Essay on the Writings and Genius of Shakespeare* held the field. Baretti could hardly hope to rival the fame of the female Mæcenas of Hill Street, whose work was, moreover, not above the heads of the average men of the day, though Johnson and Horace Walpole appreciated it at its true value. Voltaire took no notice of the attacks of the 'Aristarchus and Zoilus of Italy' at any time beyond calling him 'impertinent, pretentious and pedantic'. Not till the height of the Romantic Movement in 1820 was a poor Italian translation of the *Discours*, by Girolamo Pozzoli, published in Milan. It was not reprinted in the original French till 1911.

Baretti, however, had lived for years in England. But this was not the case with Alessandro Verri, of whom we have already spoken. A confirmed Anglomaniac, he had spent about a couple of months in London in 1766–7. At that time he did not know enough English to follow a play, though he went frequently to the theatre, so that it is not astonishing that

[1] *London Review* (1777), Vol. V. p. 531.

he says nothing about Shakespeare in his letters. But his criticisms on our acting are interesting. In comedy he considers us equal, if not superior, to the French. 'I have witnessed scenes in English comedy which, in their completeness, reach the highest point of the ridiculous and the comic.' He greatly admired Hogarth, sending his brother a set of *Marriage à la Mode.* But it is different with tragedy. He finds the dresses absurd and there is no nobility of expression. 'If two friends are to embrace, they do so like a couple of porters, hugging each other tightly round the body. When they have a set speech to make, they shout like madmen, stamp their feet and beat their breasts.' The English object to an audible prompter, yet the exit of an actor is invariably heralded by the tinkling of a bell which destroys all illusion. In fact, they are mere barbarians when compared with the French. You need Corneilles and Voltaires and actors of the grand school to produce real effect. According to Giulio Carcano, Verri saw Garrick.[1] If so, he was not impressed by him in tragedy. Garrick himself was in Italy in 1763–4. Did he entertain his friends there with the recitations of 'Is this a dagger which I see before me?' that did so much to awaken interest in Shakespeare in France?

Vincenzo Martinelli, who spent many years in London and could, of course, follow a play, had a much higher opinion of our acting. At Covent Garden he saw Mrs. Cibber imitate death so naturally in 'the tragicomedy of *Romeo and Juliet*' that, to his no small disgust,

---

[1] *Rivista Europea*, November–December, 1845.

C. Rampoldi inc

Conte Alessandro Verri

ALESSANDRO VERRI.
(From the engraving by C. Rampoldi.)

[To face p. 56.

she forced him to shed a flood of tears. Indeed, he thinks that such performances have not a little to do with the prevalence of suicide in England.[1]

Soon after his return from England, however, Alessandro Verri began to interest himself in Shakespeare. He writes to his brother Pietro (9 August, 1769) that he has translated nearly all Shakespeare's famous tragedy of *Hamlet*. 'This writer is so difficult that not even half the English understand him properly, just as few Italians understand Dante.' But he has succeeded after much trouble, 'and it is the only literal translation of this writer in existence, so far as I know. The versions in the *Théâtre Anglais* (La Place) are very free.' He does not seem to have heard of Valentini's translation of *Julius Cæsar*. Like Baretti, whose dictionary he finds excellent, he considers either that Voltaire did not understand English, or that he deliberately made Shakespeare ridiculous. 'But he was wrong, for, with all his extravagances, he was a great man.' Pietro Verri is enthusiastic over the version of 'To be or not to be', finding in it 'a force and an energy quite peculiar ; sombre colouring that produces the desired effect ; nothing exaggerated, everything being taken from Nature ; sentiments most interesting, yet harmonising with the human heart, to which tragic poets, especially the French, often fail to pay sufficient attention.' Though Alessandro had then only reached the fourth act, he ultimately finished the whole play and put *Othello* into prose as well, leaving the translations unpublished

[1] *Istoria Critica della Vita Civile* (1752), c. xiv. p. 175.

at his death. In his opinion, Italian was better able to give the sense and colouring of the original than French. He told his brother (18 April, 1778) that his own two poor tragedies, or *tentative drammatiche*, as he called them, were the result of long study of Homer and Shakespeare.[1] According to Bertana[2] the unity of place is not strictly observed, and there is a trace of romantic melancholy in *Pantea*. In the *Congiura di Milano* Verri follows history closely and 'dramatises the story with an artistic effectiveness much inferior, but not dissimilar from that of Shakespeare.' Thus in a letter he regrets being unable to kill Galeazzo Sforza in a church, such a scene being impossible in Italy, 'although not for the English who follow truth and nature in their plays and paint them in their own colours.'[3] And he proceeds to quote *Hamlet* and *Romeo and Juliet*. The play owes something to *Julius Cæsar*. Moreover, Galeazzo is not the conventional tragic tyrant of the day. He is ironical and can joke like Richard III or Iago.

But perhaps the most forcibly stated and whole-hearted vindication of Shakespeare's methods, with the exception of Baretti's, is to be found in Lorenzo Pignotti's letter to Mrs. Montagu, who had sent him her *Essay*, prefixed to his *Tomba di Shakespeare* (1779). Pignotti owes his fame largely to his Fables, which were much admired in their day. He had many English friends,

---

[1] See the letter quoted by Maggi in the Memoir prefixed to Verri's *Vicende Memorabili dal* 1789 *al* 1801.

[2] *Il Teatro Tragico Italiano del Secolo XVIII prima dell' Alfieri*, in *Giorn. Stor. Letter. Ital.* (1901), Suppl. IV. p. 99, and *La Tragedia*, p. 263.

[3] Mazzoni, *L'Ottocento*, p. 171.

but he had never been in England. 'For a long time
past the most sensible among people of taste have seen
that many of the rules laid down by the critics are
false, since they are in contradiction to nature. . . .
When the poet succeeds in moving, in delighting his
hearers by violating the rules, we must condemn the
rules and not the poet. Yet such is the force of
prejudice that cultivated readers, after weeping over
Shakespeare's tragedies and being quite carried away
by Ariosto, yet condemn the two poets, because they
sin against Aristotle's canons.' Mrs. Montagu's book
sent him back to Shakespeare, where he found ever
new beauties. Being on a holiday in the country, he
was seized with a poetic frenzy which resulted in the
Tomba di Shakespeare. The only good he claims for it
is the praise of Shakespeare and of Mrs. Montagu
which it contains.

The idea of the poem is not new, even in Italy.
Pope's shade had been invoked in a number of pieces
for various purposes, since Frugoni had started the
fashion. Pignotti himself produced an *Ombra di Pope*
(1782), in honour of the Duchess of Rutland, which
proclaimed the superiority of the English poetry of the
day over the Italian. Here, however, Pignotti is carried
to Westminster Abbey, where Shakespeare's Ghost
appears laurel-crowned upon his own monument, with
the lute 'de'cor signora', between weeping Melpomene
and winged Fancy, who touches the poet with her
wand and shows him an admirable series of pictures—
Cæsar's murder, Othello strangling Desdemona, the

Ghost in *Hamlet,* and other Shakespearean supernatural beings—Ariel raising the storm, the fairies in *Midsummer Night's Dream* and scenes from *Henry VI* and *Richard III.* Quotations from *Julius Cæsar* and *Hamlet* are interspersed, e.g.,

> Ieri un tuo cenno
> Fece tremare il mondo : oggi tu giaci
> Inonorata e sola.

> But yesterday the word of Cæsar might
> Have stood against the world, &c.—(*Jul. Cæs.,* iii. 2.)

Or

> O voi celesti
> Geni di grazia, o placidi ministri,
> Difendeteci voi.

> Angels and ministers of grace defend us !
> —(*Hamlet,* iii. 2.)

It is Shakespeare's birthday, when Apollo always visits his monument. The god now enters on a car with the Muses, in a scene obviously modelled on the divine pageant in Dante (*Purg.* 29). He is accompanied by the principal poets, Milton, Dryden, 'heir of the Theban lyre'; Pope, the singer of the 'rape of the golden lock'; Gray, 'who wept the bloody wrongs done to the sons of Parnassus'—all recent poets, one observes—and the English Roscius, 'but newly a shade'. Shakespeare mounts the car and Apollo bids 'the illustrious lady, the glory of the weaker sex, the envy of the stronger,' offer her tribute to the bard. The volume is reverently placed before him. In it, says Apollo, 'she defended thee with shields of sevenfold adamant, prepared by reason,

Dal pallido livor, che tenta invano
Con dente sparso di viperea spuma
Morder le tue grand' opre, e indarno grida
Con importuna voce, che dell' arte
Non conoscendo tu ne fren, ne legge,
Ove il folle capriccio, ove il bizzarro
Imaginar ti trasse, impetuoso
Con passo incerto, e irregolar corresti.'

But he replies that art is

Infelice
Quando a natura contrastare ardisce
E imprigionarla tenta, e farla serva,

and continues to vindicate the poet against Voltaire
and his myrmidons. The simile of the English park
and the French garden again appears, and finally the
hills of Pindus and the vocal woods—apparently we
have been wafted far from the Abbey during the speech
—echo again and again with 'Montagù! Montagù!'
Most of Pignotti's shafts come, of course, from the
quiver of the Queen of the Bluestockings, but he was
undoubtedly a genuine admirer of Shakespeare, and
his knowledge of our literature was considerable for
his day. Mrs. Montagu's famous *Essay* was translated
into Italian in 1828.

IV

SHAKESPEARE IN ITALY FROM 1790 TO 1800.

THE French Revolution had its effect even upon the position of Shakespeare in Italy, while Napoleon's Italian campaign, which resulted in the formation of the Cisalpine Republic in 1797, marks the beginning of a new epoch for the country. The last ten years of the century also saw the gradual rise of Alfieri's popularity, which was to reach its height during the Napoleonic period at the beginning of the new century. The appearance of a great tragic poet at this time to reinforce classical tradition was, of course, an important factor in counteracting the growth of Shakespeare's influence. To Germany Shakespeare came as a deliverer, and though Italy was too much under the heel of France, too classical in sympathy, ever to have been influenced by him to the same extent, it is not improbable that he would have gained ground there more rapidly if a deliverer had not arisen in Italy herself. To Alfieri it seemed as natural that tragedy should be governed by laws as the state itself, and he threw his whole weight into the scale of the traditions, which harmonized completely with his own temperament. He is, in fact, 'a French classic raised to the highest power of concentration', who carried out Voltaire's counsels of perfection as to simplicity and rapidity with a thoroughness never dreamt of by their author.

Yet Alfieri was a confirmed Anglomaniac. Like Valentini he was too impatient to learn English, though he made four attempts to do so, but England, which he knew well, was the one country that rivalled Italy in his affection. Here there were neither oppressors, nor oppressed, he declared. He grew more and more in love with British customs, and chafed more and more at the slavery of his own country. He even suggested as his epitaph :

> Securo alfin l'Italo Alfieri qui giace,
> Cui dier sol gli Angli e libertate e pace.[1]

In his letter to Calzabigi about his tragedies he says that he had been privileged to see both French and English plays acted, and he may therefore well have seen Shakespeare on the stage. In any case he knew something of him. Shakespeare was one of the great poets whose names adorned the collar with which he rewarded himself for learning Greek late in life— a charming story with which he ends his autobiography. But so afraid was he of losing his individuality that he invariably gave up reading any author by whom he thought himself likely to be seriously influenced, and 'for this reason also I gave up reading Shakespeare, to say nothing of the fact that I was obliged to read him in French. But the more strongly the writer appealed to me (mi andava a sangue), though I was well aware of his faults, the more determined was I to give up reading him ' (*Vita*, Pt. iv. chap. ii).

[1] cf. also *I Viaggi*, I and II.

There was, in fact, a strong romantic vein in Alfieri. He was an enthusiastic admirer of Ossian, and his lyrics show that the wild scenery of the North appealed to his natural melancholy. But *Saul* is the only one of his plays in which this trait appears. Indeed, Sismondi regarded it as Shakespearean rather than French in character. 'It is not a conflict between passion and duty that brings about the catastrophe. . . . It is rather a representation of a noble character who is not free from the great weaknesses which sometimes accompany great virtues.' Andrea Liruti, who spent some time in England after living through most of the phases of the Revolution, also compares Alfieri to Shakespeare, like Calzabigi :

> Tu non del prisco Acheo, del Gallo, o Ibero
> Per sentier triti ormi seguaci stampi ;
> Ma sol, duce natura, dell' altero
> Anglo Shakespeare al bollent' estro avvampi.

Alfieri himself was well aware that Saul, with his doubts and hesitations, differed in kind from the hot-headed opponent of tyranny who is usually the hero of his tragedies. Yet he gave it as his opinion that Cleopatra was a bad subject, 'non tragediable da chi si fosse' (*Vita*, Pt. IV. chap. i). However, according to Guido Mazzoni[1] he was clearly imitating Shakespeare in *Ugolino*, only fragments of which remain. Ugolino's dream while imprisoned in the tower, with its recitative and choruses, is obviously borrowed from that of Queen Catherine in *Henry VIII*.

[1] *L'Ottocento*, p. 170.

But Alfieri's influence was due rather to the gospel he preached than to his theory of tragedy. A genuine son of the didactic eighteenth century, he regarded courage in proclaiming what he believed to be the truth as the highest virtue a writer can possess. In his opinion the overthrow of tyranny came before every other duty. Like an ancient Roman, he considered monarchy to be a crime in itself, maintaining that the ideal monarch can only show his great qualities by resigning his power. It is true that he was horrified at the Revolution when it actually broke out and failed to realize the full import of his dedication of his *Bruto Secondo* 'al popolo futuro italiano'. But the fact that the political ideals of the best elements in the peninsula at this time rapidly came to coincide with the doctrines preached by Alfieri unquestionably helped for the moment to rivet the chains of Aristotle's canons more firmly upon the tragedy of the country.

As yet, however, Alfieri had not attained to a dominating position on the stage. The last years of the eighteenth century are marked by the growing popularity of the 'comédie larmoyante' in Italy. Plays of this class abound in the *Teatro Moderno Applaudito* and are an outward and visible sign of the rise to power of the middle classes, for whom Alfieri felt such unbounded contempt. This widening of the dramatic horizon and breaking down of barriers was undoubtedly calculated to bring Shakespeare a stage nearer to general recognition. Though Pierantonio Meneghelli is no enthusiast, the remarks in his *Dissertazione sopra la*

F

Tragedia Cittadinesca (1795) show clearly in which direction the tide is setting. It is true that in the text he merely says that Shakespeare put tragic stories on the stage and as long as his countrymen continue to regard them as perfect they will have but few good tragic poets (p. 15). But in a note on page 76 he tells us that though we may compare Shakespeare to Aeschylus 'for the fire, concentration and energy of his style, and the strong, virile, concise nobility of his thoughts', he is not his equal in the regularity of the structure of his plays. But we must not judge him by the rules, since he paid no heed to Aristotle ; and perhaps this is why Milton called him 'Fancy's child'. Meneghelli, in fact, had a considerable knowledge of English literature, and refers to the '*Art of Sinking in Poetry* of that celebrated Englishman Martino Scribler.' Shakespeare, however, is a conscientious follower of Nature, 'and as he knows how to inspire terror by cleverly-contrived pauses—an art now most successfully imitated by the Germans—he fills our minds with forebodings of what is about to happen by holding the action in suspense.' He has been blamed for mixing comedy with tragedy. 'But do we not every day meet people who make the tears stream from our eyes . . . and yet a moment later force us to laugh by an ill-timed joke?' This much at least Shakespeare has gained by the introduction of the *bourgeois* drama, which is the subject of Meneghelli's book.

Elisabetta Caminer-Turra (1751–96), a prolific translator and adapter of plays of this kind, and a well-known figure in the literary world of the Veneto, is generally said to have translated Shakespeare.[1] But I can find no trace of any version by her and Signorina Laura Lattes, whose *Una Letterata Veneziana del Secolo XVIII*[2] is the best account of her that has yet been published, has very kindly examined for me not only her printed works, but also her manuscripts in Vicenza, with no better success. In any case, as Elisabetta Caminer-Turra was ignorant of English, she can only have known Shakespeare in French renderings. The legend of her translation of Shakespeare probably owes its origin to her fondness for the English theatre of her day.

But Italian writers of the *comédie larmoyante* generally speak of Shakespeare with favour, though they may not display much knowledge of his works. The eccentric Count Pepoli was as eager to rival Alfieri in tragedy as in his passion for horses. In the Introduction to his *Gelosia Snaturata, ossia la Morte di D. Carlo, Infante di Spagna* (1787), he tells us that at a performance of the play in his own little theatre the audience was so profoundly moved that he was reminded of 'the god of the English stage, the divine Shakspear. Perhaps in his many defects, someone will say ; but, with this ready critic's permission, I shall not refuse to flatter myself with a different interpretation.' The similarity of the plot of Count Camillo Federici's *Duca di Borgogna, o siano I Falsi Galantuomini* to *Measure for Measure* has

---

[1] See, for instance, *Biografia degli Italiani Illustri*, Vol. V. p. 462.
[2] *Nuov. Arch. Ven.* (No. 8, 1814).

not escaped notice. The incident of the unjustly accused cashier, Danvelt, whose wife the Duke's representative would seduce after murdering her husband, were he not prevented by the Duke himself, who is travelling incognito among his people, naturally recalls Angelo's story. But the resemblance is probably fortuitous.

So Giovanni de Gamerra, perhaps the most popular of all the writers of this kind of play, boasts of uniting the boldness of a Shakespeare with the clever intrigue of a Lope de Vega in his horrible domestic tragedy of *La Madre Colpevole.* In his *Osservazioni sullo Spettacolo in generale* (1786) he says that Shakespeare allowed tragedy to appear on the stage 'without the support of the rules, but adorned by an imagination pathetic and sublime, fantastic and picturesque, gloomy and vivid. He compels our admiration, but the admiration he excites does not last long. Scenes distinguished by all the dignity and nobility of Raphael are succeeded by scenes of a vulgarity worthy of a tavern painter.'[1]

During these years, then, we find Shakespeare slowly but surely gaining ground. In dedicating his translation of the *Œdipus Tyrannus* (1796) to Prince Augustus Frederic of England, Luigi Lamberti ranks with Sophocles 'that bright luminary of the English stage, William Shakespeare who, the further he departs from the too studied regularity of modern tragic poets, the nearer does he approach the strength and vividness of the ancients.' The criticism is original and sounds sincere, though a sceptic might attach more weight to

[1] Graf, *Anglomania*, p. 322.

it if it did not occur in a dedication to an English Prince.

The younger generation was even beginning to grow familiar with Shakespeare, notably Vincenzo Monti, whose perfect taste enabled him to appreciate good poetry wherever he found it. 'I do not want anyone to think that I am more devoted to one poet than to another. I am an enthusiastic reader of all the good masters and the beauties of one do not prevent me from appreciating and admiring the beauties of another.'[1]

Not that Monti read Shakespeare in the original. Like Manzoni and most of his contemporaries he was ignorant of English and obliged to go to Le Tourneur for his knowledge. The importance of the influence of this translation can hardly be exaggerated. Leoni's Italian versions did not appear till most of the cultivated men of the day in Italy had learnt to love Shakespeare in Le Tourneur. Surely the enthusiastic admiration for Shakespeare which this by no means remarkable version was able to arouse is a strong argument in favour of the superiority of a good prose translation of a poet over a second rate rendering in verse.

Monti's tragedies, *Aristodemo* (1786) and *Galeotto Manfredi* (1788), though composed before the Revolution, belong essentially to this period. Shakespeare's contributions to the dramatic stock in trade of the time may be regarded as three in number—the introduction of ghosts, and of the People as a speaking character, and the funeral orations in *Julius Cæsar*. All of these

[1] Dedication to Mons. Ennio Quirino Visconti.

had been hallowed for the continent by Voltaire's
imitations and they all find a place in Monti's tragedies.
Dirce's Ghost plays a prominent part in *Aristodemo*.
It is more material than those of Shakespeare and can
drag Aristodemo about the stage. Its effect is not
therefore purely moral, but, as so often in Shakespeare,
it is visible to the King alone. The horror of the
King's remorse, however, owes as much to Alfieri's
Saul as to Shakespeare. But there are close verbal
parallels with *Hamlet :*—

> Se dovesse un colpo solo
> Tutti i miei mali terminar?—(iii. 1.)
> When he himself might his quietus make
> With a bare bodkin.—(iii. 1.)

Similarly, Aristodemo's comments on death in iii. 7,
often remind one of Shakespeare, and we may compare

> Oh ! se volessi io dirti
> Quant' egli è truce, ti farei le chiome
> Rizzar per lo spavento,

with

> I could a tale unfold, whose lightest word
> Would . . . make . . .
> Each particular hair to stand an end.—(*Hamlet*, i. 5.)

In *Galeotto Manfredi* Shakespeare's influence is much
more marked. Manfredi is no victim of fate, but a
romantic hero, if the word may be used to describe anyone so utterly weak, who is dominated by his passion
for Elisa. The incident of the oppressive taxes (i. 2)
is borrowed from *Henry VIII*, i. 2. Ubaldo's neglected

wife, Matilde, often recalls Queen Catherine, and there
are other reminiscences of *Henry VIII*, e.g.,

> Esulta ; il tempo è questo
> D'opprimere Zambrino

suggests Norfolk's speech (iii. 1). Zambrino bears
some likeness to Othello, and Elisa's account of her
love for Manfredi (ii. 2) is obviously borrowed from
Othello's description of the origin of Desdemona's love
for himself (i. 3). Monti has also gone to the same
play for hints for Matilde's jealousy. Compare

> Chi mi ruba il tesoro, finch' io l'ignoro,
> Non mi rende infelice.—(iv. 3.)

with

> He that is robb'd, not wanting what is stolen,
> Let him not know't, and he's not robb'd at all.—(iii. 3.)

The scene between Matilde and Zambrino (iv. 3) at
times recalls those between Othello and Iago. But
Monti has also been reading *Julius Cæsar*, as the
following parallels prove :—

> L'uom vile
> Più d'una volta mor pria di morire
> Ed una sola il coraggioso.—(iii. 9.)
> Cowards die many times before their deaths ;
> The valiant never taste of death but once.—(ii. 2.)

> Il cielo adunque anch'esso
> Congiurato è con noi. La spaventosa
> Sua sembianza feral l'opre somiglia
> Che prepariam.—(v. 4.)
> And the complexion of the element
> In favour 's like the work we have in hand,
> Most bloody, fiery, and most terrible.—(i. 3.)

> Fra il concepire e l'eseguir qualcuna
> Feroce impresa, l'intervallo è sempre
> Tutto di larve pieno e di terrore.—(i. 4.)

> Between the acting of a dreadful thing
> And the first motion, all the interim is
> Like a phantasma and a hideous dream.—(ii. 1.)

So compare

> Il tempo è questo e l'ora
> Degli atroci delitti.—(v. 2.)

with

> 'Tis now the very witching time of night . . .
> —(*Hamlet*, iii. 2.)

Again,

> Respira ancora
> L'assassin di tuo padre, e tu sei vivo?

is possibly a general reminiscence of the same play.

In *Caio Gracco* (1798–1800), Monti's last play, Opimio's speech over Emiliano's body (iv. 6) is a close imitation of Antony's funeral oration. Cornelia and Licinia (iv. 1–4), often remind one of Volumnia and Virgilia in *Coriolanus* (i. 3 and ii. 1), while Licinia owes something to Lady Percy in *Henry IV*, and still more to Portia in *Julius Cæsar*. Compare

> Per questo pianto mio,
> Pel nostro marital nodo, per quanti
> D'amor pegni ti diedi . . .—(iv. 2.)

> And upon my knees
> I charge you, by my once commended beauty . . .
> —(ii. 1.)

Similarly, the speeches of Gracco and Opimio to the People (iii. 3) and the crowds in the funeral scene are obviously imitated from Shakespeare, while M. Kerbaker has proved[1] that Monti's poem, *Invito di un Solitario ad un Cittadino* (1793), is largely taken from 'Under the greenwood tree' and 'Now, my comates and brothers in exile' in *As You Like It.*

> Qui sol d'amor sovrana è la ragione,
>> Senza rischio la vita e senz' affanno,
>> Ned altro mal si teme, altro tiranno
>>> Che il verno e l'aquilone.
>
> Quando in volto ei mi sbuffa e col rigore
>> Dei suoi fiati mi morde, io rido e dico :
>> Non è certo costui nostro nemico,
>>> Ne vile adulatore . . .

In the Prologue to his *Arminio* (1797) Ippolito Pindemonte writes :

> Là, 've il placido Avone i campi irriga,
> Giacea della Natura il figlio caro,
> Tra i fiori e l'erba. La gran madre, assisa
> Su quella sponda istessa, il volto augusto
> Svelò tutto al fanciul, che stese ardito
> Ver lei le braccia pargolette, e rise.
> Ed ella, te' questo pennelletto, disse :
> La genitrice ritrarrai con esso,
> Bambin sublime !

This is little more than a resetting of the lines on Shakespeare in Gray's *Progress of Poesy*, which Algarotti had called a 'vivissima pittura' in his letter to W. T. How (26 December, 1762) :

[1] *Shakespeare e Goethe nei versi di V. Monti.*

> Far from the sun and summer gale,
> In thy green lap was Nature's darling laid,
> What time, where lucid Avon stray'd,
> To him the mighty mother did unveil
> Her awful face. The dauntless child
> Stretch'd his little arms and smil'd.
> This pencil take (she said) . . .

But Art refused to take him to her breast, proceeds
Pindemonte, and suckle him with her milk:

> L'arte che te nudrio, saggio Addissono,
> Per cui Caton dalle Britanne ciglia
> Trasse morendo lagrime romane.

Here again Pindemonte is borrowing, this time from
Pope's Prologue to *Cato*. He knew English and England
well, and obviously thought it safest to go to English
sources for his criticisms of Shakespeare. Though the
subject of the play is the opposition between private
affection and love of one's country, it owes more to
Alfieri's *Bruto Secondo* than to *Julius Cæsar*. However,
Telgaste's speech over Baldero's dead body is another
palpable imitation of Antony's funeral oration. Moreover, the story is distinctly Ossianesque in character,
though in form it is, of course, strictly classical, like
Monti's, and, indeed, all Italian tragedies at this time.
In his *Elogio di Leonardo Targa* Pindemonte goes out
of his way to point out that it was Germany which
taught Italy to appreciate Shakespeare, 'but only to the
great detriment of good taste'.

Giovanni Pindemonte, Ippolito's brother, was a
popular playwright of the day, with a strong sense of

the theatre. His *Adelina e Roberto* (1800), for instance, introduces us to the torture-chamber of the Inquisition and shows its victims being rescued at the last moment from an Auto da Fè in a highly sensational manner. He often changes the scene at the end of an act, but the action is usually confined within twenty-four hours. Of Shakespeare he seems to have known something. *Elena e Gherardo* is a story very similar to that of *Romeo and Juliet*, founded on a novel by Bandello. But the passion bears all the marks of the sentimentality of the day. 'Il letto nuzial sarà la tomba', 'my grave is like to be my wedding-bed', is a possible reminiscence of Shakespeare, for it is probable that Pindemonte was attracted to the subject by the popularity of *Romeo and Juliet*. The play is far more romantic in colouring than the current adaptations of Shakespeare's tragedy, to which it owes nothing. Shakespearean also are the appearance of the People at the end of his *Orso Ipato* (1797), and the murder of the tyrant by the crowd. Agrippina's speech in the play of that name (1800) reads like a direct imitation of *Macbeth*:

> Quai tetre larve
> Mi veggo intorno! E quai sanguigni spettri,
> O misera Agrippina . . .
> Ombra di Claudio lurida, ti veggo.
> Ritta incontro mi stai, con bieco ciglio
> Tu mi guati, e con man scarna mi additi
> Quella mensa ferale.—(iv. 4.)

The visions in *I Baccanali* (1807) are of the same kind:

> Ombra del Padre lurida, ti vedo . . .—(iv. 5.)

So is the apparition of the Ghost in *Cianippo* (ii. 4).
The lines :

> Se tu sapessi quanto
> Chiuso nel cor mi sta, sulla tua fronte
> Sollevar sentiresti irte le chiome,
> Geleresti d'orror . . .

are as likely to have been borrowed from Monti's
imitations in *Aristodemo* as from *Hamlet* itself. Indeed,
now that Monti had set the fashion, ghosts were
rapidly becoming a recognized feature in the tragedies
of the day for symbolizing the tortures of a guilty
conscience. They played a part similar to that of
the Furies in Greek tragedy, and though they were
ultimately Shakespearean in origin, their presence in
a play no longer implies a direct acquaintance with
Shakespeare himself.

But the century was not to close without an attempt
at a systematic translation of Shakespeare. Giustina
Renier-Michiel, one of the most distinguished Venetian
hostesses of her day, took up the task. The grand-
daughter of the last Doge but one and the niece of
Ludovico Manin, the last Doge of Venice, she was
also the god-daughter of another Doge. She liked the
English, whom she called her swallows or her cranes on
account of their migratory habits, and always welcomed
them to her salon. She began her translations while still
a girl, and later on showed them to Cesarotti, who, as we
have seen, was no admirer of Shakespeare. He selected
the best of them, *Othello*, *Macbeth* and *Coriolanus*, for
publication. We do not know what the other plays

THE SALON OF GIUSTINA RENIER-MICHIEL.
(From the engraving of Tommaso Viola's drawing.)

[*To face p. 77.*]

were, but Malamanni found some fragments of a
version of *Hamlet* among her papers.[1] Venetian women
were not well educated at this time, and she was a care-
less and inaccurate writer. Hence Cesarotti corrected
the plays throughout, and the draft of an Introduction
to *Coriolanus* in his handwriting, drawn up at her request,
though she made little use of his suggestions, may still
be seen in the Museo Civico in Venice. The *Opere
Drammatiche di Shakespeare, Volgarizzate da una Cittadina
Veneta,* Tom. I, was published in Venice by Eredi
Costantini in 1798. This is generally given as the
date and it is found on the imprint of the copy in the
St. Mark's Library at Venice, but the one in the British
Museum is dated 1797. The volume contains *Othello*.
In 1798 appeared *Macbeth* and in 1800 *Coriolanus*.
'Shakspeare was passionately fond of the fair sex and
Shakspeare could really feel the love he describes so
well,' says the Introduction to *Othello*, that a woman
pays him a well-deserved tribute in translating him.
But Giustina Renier-Michiel did not know enough
English to understand Shakespeare in the original and
she merely translates Le Tourneur, who also made
Othello his first play, and from whom the notes, the
critical opinions from English writers, and the biographical details are taken. We read of Sir Tommaso
Luigi's park, and a scarcity of 'w's in the Italian fount,
which is not unknown even to-day, leaves us Narvick
as the county of Shakespeare's birth and Roure among
his editors. The translation is in prose and is not

[1] V. Malamanni, *G. Renier-Michiel, i suoi Amici il suo Tempo.*

a remarkable performance. Dandolo only praises the Preface.[1] Even her devoted admirer, Luigi Carrer, who included an account of her in his *Anello di Sette Gemme*, merely applauds her patriotism in selecting so truly Venetian a play as *Othello* for her first volume. Yet she was obviously a genuine admirer of Shakespeare, and her loyalty to her hero is proved by her indignation with a friend for likening two worthless lovers who had committed suicide in Venice to Romeo and Juliet.

These versions won her considerable fame in her day. Among Cesarotti's letters to her[2] is the draft of one for the Abate Bianchi (January, 1802), which he has rewritten for her, regretting that the information the Abate sent her about the Stratford Jubilee had arrived too late for insertion. In the course of it she exclaims, 'Long live Great Britain, where the genius of one man forms "l'ebbrezza e la delizia di un popolo!"' Ugo Foscolo presented a copy of his *Orazione per Bonaparte* to her as 'traduttrice di Shakespeare'. A Venetian noble pointed her out to Napoleon among the spectators at a review in Venice, when he visited the city in 1807. He sent for her and asked her why she was distinguished. She answered that she had made some translations of tragedies. 'Racine, I suppose?' 'Pardon me, Your Majesty, I have translated from the English.' Whereupon, with his usual good breeding, Napoleon turned his back upon her and she was armed back to her place among the spectators by her Venetian friend.

---

[1] *La Caduta della Repubblica di Venezia*, p. 154.
[2] *Cento Lettere Inedite*, p. 28.

V

SHAKESPEARE AND THE ITALIAN STAGE
BEFORE 1800

No play of Shakespeare was, of course, performed
in Italy before the end of the century. Apparently
Francesco Gritti's version of Ducis's strange moderniza-
tion of *Hamlet*, which ran for nine nights at the San
Giovanni Grisostomo Theatre in Venice during the
Carnival of 1774, was the first tragedy founded upon
Shakespeare to be given in the Peninsula. It was equally
popular elsewhere in Italy, notably at Bologna, where,
in the summer of 1795, Menichelli's performance of
Hamlet recalled the great Molé to those who had seen
him in Paris.[1] Gritti begins his Preface by saying that
'Shakespeare's *Hamlet* is still for England what, for
instance, the *Convitato di Pietra* is for Italy, that is to
say, one of the most monstrous, yet one of the most
popular of stage plays.' 'It is impossible that there
should not remain in the composition a number of
drops from the turbid source with which it is tainted,'
say the editors, and they proceed to point out the
abominations removed by Ducis. 'From what has
been said,' they conclude, 'it is clear that the merit
of Signor Ducis in greatly improving Shakespeare's
original palliates in some degree, but not altogether,

[1] *Teatro Moderno Applaudito* (1796), Vol. II.

his mistake in choosing a subject which he should have left entirely to the English stage, since it turns on a fact quite outside nature. In spite of some good qualities which distinguish it, it dazzles the vulgar instead of pleasing and instructing them and disgusts every reasonable spectator or reader.' The *Convitato di Pietra* was the famous old mask comedy from which Lorenzo da Ponte took the libretto for Mozart's *Don Giovanni.*

The poet Vincenzo Monti tells us that, without being a Shakespeare fanatic, he had shed tears in a public theatre over *Romeo and Juliet,* and gone home horror-stricken by Hamlet's passion as early as 1779.[1] At this time, indeed, *Romeo and Juliet* was the play of plays for Italy. The quick, hot blood of Italian passion is here seen at its purest and best. In *Corinne* (Bk. VII, c. 3). Madame de Stael describes the effect of an imaginary version by her heroine, in which she plays Juliet, upon a Roman audience. She probably had in mind the private performances arranged by Madame d'Epinay at the Théâtre de la Chevrette in France. Never did a tragedy produce such an effect in Italy, she says. The Romans 'disaient que c'était là véritablement la tragédie qui convenait aux Italiens, peignait leurs moeurs, ranimait leur âme en captivant leur imagination, et faisait valoir leur belle langue, par un style tour à tour éloquent et lyrique, inspiré et naturel. . . . La pièce de Romeo et Juliet, traduite en Italien, semblait rentrer dans sa langue maternelle.'

[1] Dedication to Mons. Ennio Quirino Visconti.

Count Primoli has told us how it first awakened the artist in Signora Duse when she played it on her fourteenth birthday in the amphitheatre at Verona;[1] and who does not remember La Foscarina's vivid description of her own performance of the part there in D'Annunzio's *Il Fuoco*? At Padua, Mrs. Piozzi wrote in 1785 that she was 'unlucky enough to miss the representation of *Romeo and Juliet*, which was acted the night before with great applause under the name of *Tragedia Veronese*.[2] In Vol. III of the *Teatro Moderno Applaudito* is a translation of Mercier's *Tombe di Verona* by Giuseppe Ramirez, and we are told that 'for many years this moving and interesting play, taken from Shakespeare's *Romeo and Juliet*, has been acted in the theatres of Italy with a success which should have satisfied any author. It is generally preferred to Ducis's version.' It has, of course, been brought into strict conformity with the theatrical creed of the day. It opens with Juliet awaiting Romeo on their wedding day, and ends happily, but the passion of the original has degenerated into the feeble sentimentality of the popular *comédie larmoyante* of the period. Another version was produced in Venice in 1796, and in 1799 a *Coriolano* was staged there, but we cannot say whether it was derived from Shakespeare or not.

Thanks to German influence Shakespeare was early adapted for the Italian opera, and here again *Romeo and Juliet* was the favourite. San Severino produced an opera from it in Berlin in 1773. Others were

---

[1] *Revue de Paris*, 1 June, 1897.   [2] *Observations and Reflections*, p. 225.

G

brought out by Luigi Marescalchi in Rome (1789), Foppa in Venice (1795), and G. Maldonati in Milan (1796). We find a *Hamlet* by Luigi Caruso at Florence in 1790. About the same time Lorenzo Da Ponte, in Vienna, wrote *Gli Equivoci*, founded on the *Comedy of Errors*. Shakespeare was already well known and often acted in Vienna, though the enlightened Austrian rule does not seem to have done anything to awaken interest in him in Milan, and the subject was suggested to Da Ponte by Storace. Michael Kelly, the famous Irish tenor, who was the Antipholus of Ephesus, tells us in his Memoirs that the book was excellent, and that Storace's lovely music made it very popular.

From a letter of Luigi Cerretti we learn that the Court of Parma prohibited a ballet of *Hamlet* in 1798 the day before it was to be produced there, on the ground that it was 'contaminated by conspiracies and by the death of the sovereigns.'[1] As we shall see, more than one of Shakespeare's plays was to provide a subject for a ballet during the early years of the next century.

[1] Cantù, *Corrispondenze di Diplomatici della Repubblica e del Regno d'Italia*, p. 253.

VI

SHAKESPEARE IN ITALY DURING THE NAPOLEONIC PERIOD (1800-15)

THE few months of brutal Austrian rule which followed the overthrow of the Cisalpine Republic in 1800 made Italy welcome back the French after Marengo. England in consequence, especially after Trafalgar, became the official enemy. Anglophobia took the place of the earlier Anglomania. Gioia's *Cenni Morali e Politici sull' Inghilterra estratti dagli Scrittori Inglesi* (Milan, 1806), was translated into French with the title of *L'Angleterre Jugée par Elle-Même*, and was one of the books most assiduously circulated by Napoleon with the object of fostering anti-English feeling. Monti, as always, faithfully mirrored the fashion of the hour in the sonnet *All' Inghilterra*, beginning:

> Luce ti nieghi il sole, erba la terra . . .

And this anti-English feeling left its mark upon literature generally.

In any case the classical revival encouraged by Napoleon found a congenial soil in Italy, where it helped to reinforce French classical traditions, though it had there descended in an almost unbroken line from Rome herself. Hence it is not surprising to find Alfieri rapidly attaining the zenith of his popularity. Napoleon well knew the value of the theatre in influencing public opinion. Translations of the great French tragic poets were regularly performed, and the French conquerors did everything in their power to fan the flames of this enthusiasm for Alfieri, in spite of his *Misogallo*, in which his violent hatred of the French finds full expression, owing to his republican principles and the gospel of tyrannicide which he preached. Apparently Napoleon had no fear of being regarded as a tyrant himself, at least in Italy. Alfieri's plays were almost everywhere chosen to inaugurate the new era. His *Virginia* and Salfi's notorious *Ballo del Papa* opened the Jacobin theatre in Milan, and the solemn crowning of his bust in the same theatre received official recognition.

Yet in spite of everything English books were read in increasing numbers in the peninsula, though, owing to the war, they were usually old books. During the eighteenth century the literatures of the North had, indeed, been admitted into the holy ground of classicism on sufferance. The popularity of Young and Gray and Ossian was possible because they had not definitely broken with classical tradition. But the change was inevitably coming, and even Napoleon's efforts could only keep the barbarians of the North at bay for a short while longer.

In these circumstances, however, Shakespeare did not, as was only to be expected, make much progress. Giambattista Corniani, whom Foscolo dubs 'pedante, frate, ignorante', certainly knew English, and quotes Johnson, Addison, Steele and others in his *I Secoli della Letteratura Italiana* (1804–13). He is no blind admirer of the French. 'If a day shall come when, weary at last of so much artifice and affectation, they allow themselves to be guided by Nature, like Homer, Dante and Shakespear . . . we shall say that God has touched their hearts.'[1] In talking of Giraldi Cintio's novels he says that 'the gigantic Sackespeare took from them nearly all the subjects, which he afterwards used in his tragedies with the sublimity and greatness known to the world of letters.' So the Italian should have some share in the glory given to this far-famed Englishman. And in a note he quotes 'Sackespeare's plots are in the hundred novels of Cinthio' from the Preface of Dryden's *Mock Astrologer*.[2] So of Bandello : 'Among the merits of his tragic tales we must not forget to mention that from one of them, entitled *Romeo e Giulietta*, the sublime English tragic poet Sackespeare took the subject of one of his most popular plays, which bears that name.'[3]

Monti's enthusiasm showed, of course, no sign of flagging, though he had ceased to write plays. 'Shakespeare, the great painter of ghosts, has, if we may say so, sown spectres through his tragedies and each one of them is wonderfully effective. But of all his portentous visions, none, in my opinion, so impresses the mind as the apparition of the hand grasping a dagger which is seen by Macbeth as he is on the point of entering King Duncan's room to murder him. . . . This is the hand which, mutatis mutandis, appears on Frederic the Great's sword to prevent its being removed.' So wrote Monti

---

[1] Quoted by Schiavello in *La Fama dello Shakespeare*, as Vol. V. p. 134. But I cannot identify the reference.   [2] Vol. VI. p. 253.   [3] Vol. VI. pp. 15–16.

to the aged Saverio Bettinelli, whose contemptuous
references to Shakespeare we have already mentioned,
in 1807, about his *Spada di Federico*, a poem in honour
of Napoleon in which the victor of Jena is shown
grasping Frederic's sword. Cesarotti had written to
him that the idea was one which Milton might have
envied. In this letter Monti discusses Shakespeare's
ghosts at some length, pointing out that Banquo's Ghost
and the phantom dagger are only objective images of
the thoughts that haunt Macbeth's guilty conscience.
So are the apparitions in *Julius Cæsar* and *Richard III*,
while the white-robed figures appearing to Queen
Catharine in *Henry VIII* 'are only a beautiful allegory
of the peaceful, golden dreams of a virtuous soul'.
They are visible to the Queen alone, Monti maintains,
not to the audience. Further on he says that, on first
reading the sleep-walking scene in *Macbeth*, he was
filled with horror and terror. Then only did he learn
how to 'paint the abstract ideas of the imagination
and the consequences of great crimes.'

The seventh of Monti's *Lezioni di Eloquenza* ends
with a translation of the well-known speech from the
first part of *Henry IV*, iii. 1: 'How many thousand
of my poorest subjects' . . . And he calls *Henry IV*
'one of the finest and most highly esteemed tragedies
of that supreme genius.' Nor are further imitations
wanting. In the fifth Canto of the *Bardo della Selva
Nera* (1806) the description of the effect of Napoleon's
presence in Egypt,

> Vita di tutto ei tutto osserva, e saggio
>> Dispon dell'opra il mezzo e la maniera.
>> Tale il re delle pecchie . . .

is obviously something more than a reminiscence of the Archbishop of Canterbury's famous speech in *Henry V*, i. 2, except that, as Zumbini points out,[1] Monti has gone to Virgil for the details of the description of the honey-bees. Shakespeare is fond of comparing the functions of kingship to those of the sun, and the long passage in the next canto:

> Delle stelle monarca egli s'asside
>> Sul trono della luce, e con eterna
>> Unica legge il moto e i rai divide
>> Ai seguaci pianeti e li governa . . .

is almost a paraphrase of Ulysses's speech in *Troilus and Cressida*, i. 3 :

> The heavens themselves, the planets and their centre
> Observe degree, priority and place . . .

Again,

> Tra la primiera genitrice idea
> Di perigliosa impresa ed il momento
> Dell' eseguire, l'intervallo è tutto
> Fantasmi, e bolle de' pensieri il flutto.
>> Allor fiera consulta in un ristretti
>> Fan dell'alma i tiranni ; e la raccolta
>> Raggion nel mezzo ai ribellati affetti
>> Sta qual re tra feroci arme in rivolta,

in Canto vi is another development of

> Between the acting of a dreadful thing . . .

---

[1] *Sulle Poesie di Vincenzo Monti*, p. 137.

In Canto vii

> Aleggiar sento del giorno
> L'aura vietata che m'incalza

recalls

> But soft! Methinks, I scent the morning air,

of the Ghost in *Hamlet*, i. 5. Again,

> Qual veggiam talvolta, o veramente
> Avvisiam di veder per le notturne
> Ombre gli spettri abbandonar le tombe,
> E vagar per le case e per le vie,

in *Prometeo* (Canto iii), another of Monti's Napoleonic poems, is clearly a reminiscence of *Julius Cæsar*, ii. 2. Lastly, to anticipate a little, in a letter to Tedaldi-Fores (30 November, 1825) he speaks of 'Schiller who, after Shakespeare, is far more my love than yours.'

Monti habitually read with a grappling-hook, and the passages he has imitated were doubtless to be found in his wonderful common-place book. But he was unquestionably the most genuine admirer of Shakespeare among the poets of Italy before Manzoni, and we have here ample proof of the thoroughness of his knowledge of Shakespeare's works in Le Tourneur's translation. Nor was his enthusiasm likely to be diminished by the friendship he formed with Madame de Stael during her first visit to Italy in 1804–5. But even the presence of this disinguished victim of Napoleon, accompanied by A. W. von Schlegel himself as tutor to her boys, did not at this time do much to awaken interest in the literature of the North, brilliant though her reception had everywhere been.

Ugo Foscolo, the other great poet of this period, classed Shakespeare with Alfieri, Sophocles and Voltaire as a tragic poet to be studied, as early as 1796, but his tragedies contain no sign that he had studied him himself. Yet for all his classical sympathies there was an even profounder romantic strain in Foscolo than in his master Alfieri. It is most marked in his novel *Le Ultime Lettere di Jacopo Ortis*, the hero of which declares that 'Homer, Dante and Shakespeare, three masters of all the super-human geniuses, have possessed my imagination and fired my heart.' Not that Foscolo was ever a Shakespeare enthusiast. In the Introduction to his translation of the *Sentimental Journey*, which he began while serving as an officer with Napoleon's army of invasion at Boulogne, he says that 'Shakespeare is like a forest on fire, making a fine display at night, but sending forth only smoke by day'. Gamerra has borrowed this simile in the Preface to his *Madre Colpevole*—already quoted—when he compares Shakespeare's beauties to bright sparks scattered among clouds of black smoke.

At this time, however, Foscolo was learning English, and though he had no sympathy with the romantic school, he soon began to appreciate Shakespeare. In a letter of 1805 he writes, 'Vous savez que j'ai rencontré l'histoire de mon amour infortuné dans une des tragédies de Shakespeare.

> She lov'd me for the dangers I had pass'd
> And I lov'd her that she did pity them.'[1]

[1] *Opere*, Vol. VI. p. 55.

Was he referring to the English lady who about this time became the mother of his daughter Floriana? We do not know, but his letters prove that he soon obtained a good knowledge of English.

In a letter to Count Giambattista Giovio (1 May, 1809) he asks, 'Who does not see the faults and extravagances of Dante and Shakespeare? Yet who does not feel his mind broadened and ennobled by reading these sublime authors?'[1] Again, when writing to Lord Dacre during his exile in England (14 January, 1823) he quotes 'To be or not to be', and in another letter to his friend and benefactor Hudson Gurney, written in the year before his death (12 August, 1826), he compares his sleepless state to that of Lady Macbeth. He was also well aware of the growing popularity of Shakespeare in Italy. Leoni sent him his translations and asked him for his opinion upon them, but no letter of his in answer has been preserved. In his *Saggio della Letteratura Italiana*[2] he bids his readers not to be astonished at Young's popularity in Italy, 'since the works of Shakespeare and Milton in the original are most highly esteemed', being studied and enthusiastically admired by the most cultivated young men and women in the peninsula. These remarks, however, belong to a rather later period than that with which we are here concerned.

Interesting signs of the times are the essays prefixed by Ippolito Pindemonte to the third edition of his *Arminio* (1812), which were actually written in 1804.

[1] *Opere*, VI. p. 255.   [2] *Ib.*, XI. p. 215.

He has been guilty of an offence for which he will not in all probability be pardoned, he tells us. He has observed the rules of tragedy in his play. 'What servility, superstition, cowardice!' The prevailing spirit of licence, which has overrun everything, has spread even to literature, he declares. 'Moreover,' he continues in the second Essay, 'the fame enjoyed at present by the English Shakespeare in Europe has encouraged this audacious freedom, so damaging to letters; if we ought not rather to say frankly that the prevailing state of feeling contributed not a little to the vogue of that poet of the North. . . . Not a few of those vaunted flowers of beauty would please less, if they grew in a field less wild.' In England most of the best judges speak of him with a moderation which foreigners would do well to imitate. Hume, Blair and Mason are no enthusiasts, while Addison and Milton obey the unities. 'If, as is admitted, taste does not abound in Shakespeare's brain, and if he cannot be adopted as a model, I shall conclude that he did not possess true genius, though it is contrary to the general opinion.' His subjects show no power of invention, and his ignorance of the rules, which were observed by Ben Jonson, if real, need not have prevented him from discovering them for himself, like the Greeks, if he had possessed the necessary taste. The fact that he could move his characters from place to place and display them in the vulgarest surroundings gave him a great advantage over the regular dramatist who has no such privileges. 'In spite of all this, I am quite

ready to admit that his pictures are often marvellous.'
Pindemonte does not deny that the rules of art may
be violated, but he insists that this can only be done
with success when they are perfectly known and understood.

In 1811, however, appeared in Milan, *Saggi di Eloquenza Estratti dal Teatro di Shakespeare*. 'The popular
idea of Shakespeare among us', says the Preface, 'is that
he is a sublime painter of terrible images. Yet no poet
at any time possessed a genius of wider range than
Shakespeare's. . . . Being desirous of giving some idea
of the beauties of every kind in this supreme poet,
I have selected some highly eloquent passages from
his plays and decided to publish them.' But here again
it is to Le Tourneur that the writer has gone for his
knowledge and he apologizes for offering mere retrans-
lations to his readers, thus showing them Shakespeare
through a double veil. The versions are certainly very
free. They are, of course, in prose.[1] To the same year
also belongs the first of Michele Leoni's verse translations of Shakespeare, *Julius Cæsar*, published by G. G.
Destefanis in Milan.

On the other hand we may note that Luigi Cerretti,
in his *Istituzioni di Eloquenza*, also of 1811, which was
a popular school book in its day, considers that frequent
changes of scene are fatal to probability, 'as in the
famous *Othello* of Shakespeare, the English Sophocles,
a barbarous play which is beloved even in our time by
that ferocious nation and in which the first scene is in

---

[1] For the contents of this volume, see Appendix.

Venice, the last in Cyprus' (p. 173). One remembers that this is the very instance chosen by Johnson to justify Shakespeare's neglect of the unity of place. Francesco Reina is a little more comforting in his *Life of Parini*, which was issued in the same year. Parini's poems will, he considers, always be of value as pictures of the life of his day. In this he is 'like Homer, Horace, Dante and Shakespeare, who will always live on the lips of men as supreme historians and poets.' Shakespeare is once more in good company, we are glad to observe.

Another comparison for which there is some justification is that between Shakespeare and Metastasio, who, as we have seen, paid no more attention to the precious rules than his English predecessor, and was thought to have gone direct to nature for his inspiration. In a sonnet, *In Morte del Metastasio*,[1] the Abate Gaetano Golt shows us Artino (Metastasio) in the Elysian Fields. There he is welcomed by Sophocles and Euripides, who exclaim :

> Diasi al Greco cotorno il primo onore,
> Ma il forte Seckpaire [*sic*] e il dolce Artino
> Conobber più di noi le vie del cuore.

In the Errata (p. 350) Seckspaire is given as the correct spelling.

In the reviews of the period which we have examined we can find no reference to the book of extracts, but Leoni's translation of *Julius Cæsar* is discussed at some length in the *Giornale Enciclopedico di Firenze* for 1811

---

[1] *Poesie Scelte* (Florence, 1804), p. 250. I am indebted for my information to the kindness of Senator Guido Mazzoni, who refers to the sonnet on p. 170 of his *Ottocento*.

(Vol. III, p. 306). Filippo Irenico, the writer of the article, says that the sublime English poet, who is little read, though he deserves to be widely read, is well worthy of being translated into Italian. He refers to Giustina Renier-Michiel's versions, but says that he did not know English when he read them and now he has mislaid them. On the whole he thinks that *Julius Cæsar* has been 'excellently translated' by Leoni, who will, he hopes, continue the task upon which he has entered. He trusts that Leoni will not resent the criticisms which he is about to make, and which are worth reading, even to-day. English poetry is rich in imagery, but is often harsh in comparison with Italian poetry. 'The abundance of monosyllables gives it wonderful energy when it is required to express unusual ideas, because its sublimity then increases in proportion to the simplicity, rapidity and conciseness of the words.' It is 'superior to French poetry so far as the inflection of the phrases is concerned', but less flexible than Italian, in which it is hard to reproduce its effects. For instance :

> *Brutus.* Porzia morì.
> *Cassius.*   Chi ? Porzia ?
> *Brutus.*   Sì ; ella è morta.

'She is dead' has a noble ring in English, but in the Italian it is merely commonplace. This critic thinks that the scene between Brutus and Cassius (Act iv, sc. 3) is perhaps the best in the play, with the exception of the funeral scene, and he considers Leoni's translation of it so good that it will establish his reputation. Though it would now be generally agreed that Leoni's translation is here overrated, the criticism is distinctly above the average of the day, at least so far as Shakespearean criticism in Italy is concerned.

The *Giornale Enciclopedico* had already twice mentioned Shakespeare among distinguished English poets in this volume (pp. 33, 72), and in 1814 (Vol. VIII. p. 64) it announces its intention of giving its readers verse translations of some of the most famous passages in Shakespeare, especially the soliloquies which, in the opinion of the best judges, 'generally display more variety and sublimity in the images and more fire in the passion.' 'To be or not to be' is the first chosen, and Voltaire's version, which is deservedly censured, is included, as well as others by Crudeli and Leoni himself, who is the writer of these papers. Crudeli's rendering, now published for the first time, does not follow the usual order, but is not without merit. Leoni's version is well known. We may mention that in Vol. I of the *Raccoglitore* (1819) there is another verse translation of the same soliloquy, signed 'D. B.', which is probably, therefore, by Davide Bertolotti, the editor.

On page 131 other passages from *Hamlet* are given in Leoni's translation:

Oh, that this too, too solid flesh would melt . . . —(i. 2), and

Oh, my offence is rank, it smells to heaven . . . —(iii. 3), as well as the scene between Hamlet and his mother (iii. 4). *Macbeth* is the next play chosen (p. 288).

Act i, scenes 5 and 7 are given in their entirety, as well as 'Is this a dagger' (ii. 1).

Neither *L'Ape* (Florence, 1804–6), nor the *Giornale della Società d'Incoraggiamᵒnto delle Scienze e Belle Arti Stabilita in Milano* (1808–9) mention Shakespeare, but *La Vespa*, which succeeded the *Ape Italiana* in Milan (1807–8), contains a translation of Goethe's criticisms on *Hamlet*. The popular Milanese rival of the *Giornale Enciclopedico*, the *Poligrafo* (1811–4), merely refers to Shakespeare once in a letter to L. de Brême, which is appended to a translation of Gray's *Ode on the Spring*. In this it is said that Gray occupies the same place in English lyric poetry that Shakespeare holds in dramatic. Both the *Poligrafo* and the *Giornale Enciclopedico* ceased to exist with the fall of Napoleon and the establishment of the new order of things.

This was not the case, however, with the *Corriere delle Dame*, published in Milan, which had a long and prosperous career before it. The *Moda di Francia* is naturally the principal topic in its pages, but literature is by no means neglected and we have found several references to Shakespeare in the volumes we have searched (1810–17). The writer of some reflections on Racine and Alfieri (1810, p. 333) notes that, in spite of 'Addisson's' praise in the *Spectator*, the English translations of Racine were never popular upon our stage. The English always prefer 'the rough and irregular productions of Shakespeare, because at least they are full of movement and fire and tragic vigour and contain a number of sublime passages. Racine's frigid eloquence does not come within many miles of them.' Similarly, in 1811 (p. 75) a writer, speaking of Alfieri, says that 'Homer, Jhakespeare [*sic*] and Corneille himself, though not without very grave defects, rank above all other poets, because they aimed at the sublime rather than at the beautiful.' The *Corriere delle Dame* reflects the new tendencies in a number of articles on German literature, but in 1813 it followed the example of the *Giornale Enciclopedico* by beginning to give now and then prose versions of passages from Shakespeare. On page 84 we find 'The World compared to a Stage, a thought taken from Shakespeare', which is, of course, a translation of 'All the world's a stage'. Then, on page 239, is 'The web of our life is of a mingled yarn' from *All's Well That Ends Well* (iv. 3). The next volume (p. 172) contains the opening lines on peace in the first part of *King Henry IV*. These passages imply a considerable knowledge of Shakespeare, for they are none of them taken from the plays usually read in Italy at this time, or even in our own day.

H

VII

But the Romantic Movement was already dawning in
Italy. Madame de Stael's *Corinne* had been published in
1807, and in 1813 appeared her *De L'Allemagne,* which
Napoleon refused to allow to be printed in France. It
was eagerly devoured throughout Europe, but nowhere
more so than in Italy, where it first introduced the
word Romantic. An Italian translation was published
in the following year. The French invasion had at first
been eagerly welcomed as encouraging the nationalist
movement, but its oppressive character had ended by
strengthening that very spirit of patriotism, the absence
of which had made it so easy. The restoration of
foreign rule in the North by the Congress of Vienna
only served to turn this patriotic feeling into a new
channel. French claims to hegemony in literature had
failed as ignominiously as in politics, and it was by her
application of the theories of the Revolution to art
that Madame de Stael had declared herself an enemy
of the pretensions of her country. Literature, she
maintained, must be as free as man. All nations have
a right to intellectual equality, and she recommended the
study of the literatures of the North as best calculated
to provide the necessary stimulus. Upholders of the

classical traditions were naturally indignant, but these ideas came as a revelation to the future leaders of the Romantic Movement in Milan, which was even at this period the intellectual centre of the peninsula. Hence her second visit to Italy, when she was accompanied as before by A. W. von Schlegel, whose lectures on dramatic literature were beginning to be known beyond the Alps, was an event of the utmost importance. At Milan, Count Confalonieri, and above all Ludovico de Brême, were her enthusiastic admirers, while, in Florence, Michele Leoni spent all the time he could spare from his English friends at her feet.

Nor is it long before we begin to see the results of the change. An Italian translation of the French *Spectateur* was published in Milan, and Vol. III (1815), contains a violent attack on Shakespeare by Le Jay in his *Discorso sul Genere Romantico in Letteratura*, the comments upon which by the Italian translator are noteworthy. Shakespeare's beauties are the more striking because they are so rare; 'in French eyes,' adds the translator's note. Another note on page 159 says that 'for the instruction, as well as for the amusement of the Italian reader we are translating with special care the French version of the balcony scene from *Romeo and Juliet*'; and he is referred to Leoni's translations of Shakespeare, which were then appearing, if he would see how different is 'the burning, heroic passion with which Shakespeare endows his characters' from the caricature that results from an affectedly literal rendering of the text into another tongue. Moreover, the

Italian supplement (p. 82) contains a glowing eulogy of Shakespeare in its review of Leoni's translation, which was to embrace the eight most poetical plays. In Shakespeare poetry is not an art, but an inspiration as genuine as the Sibyl's prophecies. Before him all other tragic poets must veil their heads. His violations of the unities and his mingling of tragedy and comedy are also defended, while a short account of his life is given on page 114. We could hardly hope to meet with more whole-hearted enthusiasm.

Metternich thought that he could make capital out of the new movement by founding a review which should increase Austrian influence by encouraging an interest in German literature. The *Biblioteca Italiana* was therefore started in Milan under the editorship of Acerbi, who persuaded Madame de Stael to send him something for the first number. In her historic article *Sulla Memoria e l'Utilità delle Traduzioni* (January, 1816) she blamed Italians for their want of earnestness and expressed her belief that the best cure for the wretched state of literature in the country was to be found in translations of recent English and German poets. She did not mean that these poets were to be slavishly imitated, but pleaded that by becoming acquainted with them Italians would be able to introduce a much-needed novelty into their literature. Thanks to Schlegel's translations, Shakespeare and Schiller were played like fellow-countrymen in Germany. Why was not the same thing possible in Italy? This article naturally produced a number of replies, notably one in the April

number of the *Biblioteca Italiana* by Gherardini, urging
a return to the classics as the true remedy. Gherardini
was soon to defend Italian tragedy against Schlegel's
strictures in the notes to his translation of the lectures
on dramatic poetry, which appeared in 1818. Madame
de Stael replied to her critics, explaining her meaning
more fully, in the June number. 'A man of letters in
Florence', says she in the course of her remarks, 'has
made a profound study of English literature and has
undertaken a complete translation of Shakespear, since,
incredible though it may seem, there exists as yet no
translation of that great man. . . . But does he receive
the encouragement and credit he deserves?'

The allusion is, of course, to Michele Leoni, who was
carrying out Madame de Stael's advice with unflagging
zeal. This Hercules of Translators, as the *Conciliatore*
(No. 44) calls him, was now busy upon *Paradise Lost*.
Thomson's *Seasons*, *The Essay on Man*, some *Ossian*,
the *School for Scandal*, Hume's *History of England*, and
Byron's *Lament of Tasso* were among the other translations that flowed from his facile pen. He even found
time to write two poor tragedies, *Ifigenia* and *Il Duca
d'Enghien* (1815), on strictly classical lines.

A far greater disciple of Madame de Stael was, however, Giacomo Leopardi, whose *Pensieri* are full of
quotations from and criticisms of her writings. Unlike
her, he ranked the drama below the epic and the lyric,
because the poet loses more of his individuality in it. He
knew some English. He was acquainted with Addison,
Pope, Hervey and above all with Ossian. But we cannot

believe that he was at all familiar with Shakespeare, even in translations, in spite of his admiration for Madame de Stael. *Hamlet* could hardly have failed to appeal to one of his temperament, and his references to Shakespeare would certainly have been very different from the casual allusions in the *Pensieri*, if he had ever read him attentively. It is true that Leopardi quotes Shakespeare in support of his theory that a nation which has produced a really supreme genius in any branch of literature rarely produces another master in the same field,[1] and calls him 'a truly national writer.'[2] But he also repeats Voltaire's remark about no scene of his crossing the sea, whereas passages of the *Pastor Fido* are known by heart in Stockholm and St. Peters-burg,[3] and he blames him for his use of soliloquies. In speaking of Milton he refers to Andres's book, though he quotes 'Amongst unequals no society',[4] so that is it possible that he took Shakespeare at Voltaire's and Andres's value. However that may be, he seems to have known less of Shakespeare than most of his distinguished contemporaries. Thus we find his friend and adviser, Pietro Giordani, writing in a letter of 7 February, 1818[5]: 'I am now reading something I have long wanted to read and I am thoroughly satisfied. I am reading Shakespeare's plays, which seem to me to be a new dramatic world, and as in a world I find something of everything ; very great beauties and its share of miseries ; but we must allow

[1] *Pensieri*, II. 195.   [2] *Ib.*, IV. 51.   [3] *Ib.*, II. 153.   [4] *Ib.*, IV. 192.
[5] *Opere*, Vol. IV. p. 15.

that the beauties are great and new. And it appears to me that anyone who could make use of them might achieve great glory thereby. But, as is usual with great writers, it is the defects that are imitated.'

But it soon became evident that Metternich was grievously mistaken. Romanticism, in spite of its German origin, was to be the creed of the younger generation, which was inspired by nationalist ideals learnt during the French domination and was bitterly opposed to the return of the Austrians. Hence the *Biblioteca Italiana* was obliged to change its policy. Then in 1818 the *Conciliatore* was founded by the young Romantics, Silvio Pellico being the principal editor. It definitely threw down the glove to the old order of things. In the sphere of literature the unities occupied almost the same position as Austrian rule in the sphere of politics. They were fetters that must be broken at all costs. To men of this stamp Shakespeare was, of course, a gonfalon, and the writers in the *Conciliatore* were thoroughly familiar with his work, or at least with Le Tourneur's translation. 'I mean that if Shakespeare's *Othello*,' writes Pellico (No. 2), 'with all its characters and all its violations of the unities of time and place, excites pity and terror, it is a tragedy as true and genuine as if it produced the same effect with three characters and all the most venerated unities strictly observed.' A work of art must be judged on its merits and not in accordance with its conformity to a type. If the Romantics 'like to see witches and sorceresses in Shakespeare and Ariosto,' says Berchet (No. 17), 'they never urged

living poets to introduce them into their works after
they have ceased to live in the belief of the people.'
Ermes Visconti often mentions Shakespeare in the
series of articles on Romanticism which were afterwards published separately. He points out that it is
a mistake to suppose that Shakespeare is always gloomy.
'Shakespeare showed us Desdemona's death on the
stage, but he is also the poet of Miranda's happy
love.' (No. 27.) 'Shakespeare wrote the greatest things
that have ever been seen on the stage.' 'The scene of
Lady Macbeth's sleep-walking is one of the sublimest
that has ever been written.' If the duration of the play
is limited to twenty-four hours, you do not allow space
for the development of character, which does so much
to make the magnificent climax what it is. So says
Ermes Visconti in the dialogue on the unities (No. 42).
In the second of his *Sermoni sulla Poesia*, which have been
called the Poetics of Romanticism in Italy, Giovanni
Torti describes how 'the scholar and the merchant and
the rough sailor' in the frozen climes of Arthur sit
spell-bound while Macbeth and his wife chill them
with horror, brought upon the stage by 'il maggior
Britanno'. And he goes on to give a long and vivid
description of the sleep-walking scene. The articles on
English literature in the *Conciliatore* are well-informed,
showing a knowledge of Scott, Rogers and Byron.
Most of them are by Pellico. He expresses regret that
Campbell did not include Shakespeare in his *Specimens
of the English Poets* (Nos. 108 and 112).

Indeed, Shakespeare seems to have come as a revelation to Pellico, just as he did to Niccolò Tommaseo, who was to be one of the leading Romantic critics of the next generation, at a later date, in 1821. 'Do you remember the effect the reading of Shakespeare and Schiller had upon us?' writes Pellico to his brother on 11 December, 1815. 'How the horizon grew more vast before us? Cold reflection, the thundering voices of the pedants, often made me ask, Will this enthusiasm of mine prove to be the wayward madness of the inexperience of youth?' Then he read Sismondi and Schlegel, and once more the fire that Shakespeare and Schiller had kindled flared up in his heart.[1] Moreover, Pellico was the first romantic dramatist in Italy. His *Francesca da Rimini* (1815), in spite of its defects, can at least claim to have achieved the stage success denied to so many poetical tragedies. But it appeared before the new movement had gathered strength and strictly follows the rules, though the style is highly romantic in colouring. Nor is there any trace of Shakespeare's influence.

The playwrights, in fact, are still loyal to Alfieri to a man, even the improvisers of tragedy, who were a feature of the period which at least proves the importance attached to the drama in popular estimation, such as Tommaso Sgricci and Luigi Carrer. Yet they were becoming acquainted with Shakespeare, or at least with Le Tourneur, and were quite ready to show him how his plays ought to have been written.

[1] Rinieri, *Della Vita e delle Opere di Silvio Pellico*, Vol. I.

Giuseppe Lugnani is the author of a *Macbet,* published
in the second volume of his tragedies (1817), in which
Shakespeare's play is reduced to strict conformity with
the sacred canons. At least it owes nothing to Ducis.
It opens according to rule at the culminating point of
the story. Malcolmo is introduced into the palace at
night, ten years after Macbet has been on the throne,
to meet Olinda, the tyrant's niece, with whom he is in
love. He is at the head of the English army of revenge,
being urged on by the ghost of his murdered father
Donaldo, who shakes his gory locks at him, like
Banquo's in Shakespeare. Ango, the captain of the
Guard, who has admitted him, describes all the atrocious
deeds in which Malvina (Lady Macbeth) is the prime
mover. Malcolmo now informs Olinda of Macbet's
real character, of which she is ignorant, and she departs
in an agony of tears. In Act II we see Macbet haunted
by remorse, but encouraged by Malvina, who despises
his weakness. The murder of Banco is announced
during a Council of War, and at the sight of his ghost
on the throne Macbet falls down in a dead faint.
Olinda and Ango comment on the scene. This act is
full of echoes of Shakespeare, e.g.,

> Ben fu la serpe
> Schiacciata, non già morta.

> Donaldo è in tomba,
> Scevro dai mali di quassuso ei dorme.

> Ciò che ad uomo s'addice
> Io senza tema imprendo ; e non è uomo
> Che di più imprende ; ah ! non.

This feeble 'ah! non' is symbolic of the whole tragedy. The witches' prophecies have become a vision, and a new vision concerning Birnam wood and the other prophecies in Shakespeare makes Macbet utterly fearless when he hears of the advance of the troops. Meanwhile Malcolmo is taken prisoner and kept as a hostage, Malvina holding back the weeping Olinda when he is dragged off to prison. Next Catnesso brings the news of the murder of Macduffo's family. Ango suggests that he should make away with Malcolmo, for fear that the news of his imprisonment should rouse the people. Macbet consents. Then Olinda comes in with an account of Malvina's sleep-walking.

Act V opens with Ango announcing Malcolmo's murder, which Macbet regrets. Olinda appears with the news of Malvina's death, and Catnesso with an account of the moving wood, and of a revolt among Macbet's troops, at the head of which is Macduffo, who is determined to avenge Malcolmo. The rebels are in possession of the palace. Ango shows his true colours and arrests Macbet, who kills himself, as becomes a tyrant in this type of play, on the appearance of Malcolmo, now released from prison. Macduffo's birth fulfils the last of the prophecies. The play abounds in reminiscences of Shakespeare.

More interesting is Francesco Benedetti, who committed suicide in 1821 to escape prosecution for his dealings with the Carbonari. He was no blind follower of Alfieri, whom he blames in his *Intorno al Teatro Italiano* for the monotony resulting from his exclusion of all subordinate characters and for the want of tenderness in his tragedies. But he is infinitely more severe on Shakespeare, 'who introduces as many as thirty-eight characters into a tragedy, laying the scene of the action now in Rome, now in Modena, now in Greece. Tribunes talk with carpenters and shoemakers; there are two or three different actions; the tragedies last as long as three of ours with ghosts, furies, fairies, prose and verse, laughter and tears, and a combination of the strangest and most heterogeneous material.' Benedetti was, in fact, a thorough Voltairian. In a note he refers contemptuously to the churchyard scene and the five deaths in *Hamlet* and to Othello strangling Desdemona. 'This kind of thing may give pleasure to the English and the Germans and to people altogether Northern; but we who possess a more refined sense of beauty, who love to imitate Nature when she is noble, not when she is uncouth, can have no sympathy with such abuse of imagination, such improbabilities and, to speak plainly, such indecencies.' Similarly, in his second letter to Count Napione (7 January, 1819), he says that 'Voltaire, who had to do with Parisians, who are even more refined than we are in questions of propriety on the stage, did not reproduce *Othello*, but from that shapeless sketch (informe abbozzo) took his *Zaïre*,' which was, in Benedetti's opinion, the most moving of modern tragedies and the only one that could be said to rival those of the ancients.

Benedetti's *Druso* proves that he was familiar with Shakespeare and not above borrowing from him as early as 1813. The scene between Tiberio and Druso (ii. 6) obviously owes not a little to the well-known scene between the Prince and his father in the second part of *Henry IV*, iv. 4, and he seems to have taken hints from Shakespeare for Sejano. We also find ghosts of the usual Shakespearean kind in *Mitridate* (1809), ii. v, and *Tamerlano* (1816), ii. 3, while in *Timocare* (1817) Arsinoe's first interview with her husband after the departure of the conspirators (i. 3) is obviously modelled on that between Portia and Brutus in *Julius Cæsar*.

But his handling of Richard III in a tragedy of his own (1819) is the best proof of his disapproval of Shakespeare's methods. It begins, of course, at the culminating point, containing only the last two scenes of Act IV and the fifth act of Shakespeare's great play. There are fewer echoes of him than in Lugnani's *Macbet*. Oxford and Stanley are discussing the prospects of Richmond, who is driven back by contrary winds. Anna, Richard's queen, loves him still, though he is paying court to Isabella, daughter of Queen Isabella, who is in love with Richmond. Her mother is horrified at the news and gives an account of Richard's misdeeds, including a blood-curdling description of the murder of the Princes in the Tower, of which she was an eye-witness. In the second act Richard tells Norfolck, his confidant, of the ghosts of his victims which haunt him, and appears as the bullying, brutal tyrant in the scene with Anna, whom he commits to the Tower. Then he sends for Queen Isabella, and their interview contains some touches of Shakespeare. At her mother's

suggestion, Isabella promises Richard to marry him after
the battle. There are signs of a popular revolt, and in
a soliloquy Richard declares that he loves no one and
has no human feelings. He makes an attack upon the
English people which reflects the Anglophobia of the
day and probably represents Benedetti's own feelings.

> Che temi tu dal popolo britanno?
> Non saprei dir se più superbo o stolto,
> Porta il regale ed il patrizio giogo : . . .
>   Libero in detti,
> In opre schiavo . . .
> Sprezza ogni gente : l'universo crede
> Nato per se ; degli altrui ceppi è lieto,
> Ne i suoi conosce . . .—(iii. 6.)

In Act IV we see him in a state of utter nervous
collapse at the visions which haunt him and which owe
something to *Macbeth.* His behaviour is hardly sane
and he is only saved from worse excesses by Norfolck.
Isabella enters and tells him she would rather die than
marry him. He would have killed her on the spot, had
not Norfolck bidden her fly, and her mother meets with
no better reception. But he recovers and we see him
making his arrangements for the battle.

In the last act Norfolck appears with orders for the
murder of Isabella to prevent her from falling into
Richmond's power, but a false report of Richmond's
defeat stays his hand. Richard is then brought in
wounded and furious that the women have not been
killed, when his wife Anna suddenly drops down dead
in front of him from the effects of the poison he had

given her, just before he dies himself. In fact, Shakespeare's Richard III has degenerated in Benedetti's
hands even more than Macbeth in Lugnani's. It is
impossible to feel anything but contempt for anyone at
once so weak and so insanely cruel.

Yet time took its revenge even upon Benedetti. In
his last play, *Cola di Rienzo* (1820), which is strongly
liberal and anti-clerical, the scene is frequently changed,
though it is always in Rome. There are fourteen
characters and the unity of time is broken. Moreover,
the People appears as a speaking character, a sure sign
of Shakespeare's influence. Colonna's words in the first
scene :

> Che fate qui, gente oziosa e vile?
> Itene ai vostri giornalieri uffici,

is an obvious imitation of the first scene of *Julius Cæsar*.
Had he lived Benedetti's development might have
followed the same lines as Niccolini's and brought him
into harmony with the so-called romantic school of the
day.

But if the story of Shakespeare in Italy centres round
the name of Voltaire during the eighteenth century, it
centres no less inevitably round that of Manzoni in the
nineteenth. For Manzoni Shakespeare and Virgil were
the greatest poets. 'Anyone who wants to write must
read Shakespeare. How he understands all our feelings !'
said he once in the Countess Maffei's drawing-room.[1]
Elsewhere he is 'grande ed unico poeta.'[2] His genius

---

[1] Barbiera, *Il Salotto della Contessa Maffei*, p. 268.
[2] *Op. Var.*, p. 505.

is 'superhuman',[1] and Manzoni talks of 'Macbeth and many other divine tragedies'.[2] He made his profession of faith in a letter to Claude Fauriel (28 March, 1816) about his *Carmagnola*. 'It extends over a space of ten years. This is a terrible outrage against the rule of the unity of time, but you will be the last person to be scandalized on that account. After having carefully read Shakespeare and something of what has been recently written upon the theatre, and after thinking it all over, my views on certain reputations have undergone considerable modification.'

There are numerous references to Shakespeare in Manzoni's prose writings. In his important *Lettre à M. Chauvet sur l'Unité de Temps et de Lieu dans la Tragédie*, he contrasts *Othello* with *Zaïre* as an argument against the unity of time, showing that the former is probable because Shakespeare has taken all the time necessary for the gradual development of Othello's jealousy under Iago's diabolical influence, whereas *Zaïre* is not, because Voltaire is obliged to trust to chance owing to the action being compressed into twenty-four hours. Like Coleridge he had a profound admiration for *Richard II*. He is well aware that it is not one of the best of the historical plays; but, like Coleridge, he sympathized instinctively with the weaknesses of the unhappy king, since he felt that they were to a great extent his own. Richard's 'intellectual femineness', of which Coleridge talks when discussing the play, is a characteristic common to both poets. Manzoni examines the play carefully to

[1] *Op. Ined.*, III. p. 172.   [2] *Ib.*, p. 187.

[*To face p.* 112.

ALESSANDRO MANZONI.

show how it would have been spoilt by being constructed on classic lines. 'Marvellous Shakespeare', he exclaims. 'If only these beauties of your god-like intellect remained, what rare things would they not be considered! But your brain was able to plumb the depths of the human heart so profoundly that such beauties are common in your works.'[1]

Not that Manzoni followed Shakespeare in the structure of his own plays, which differ little from the classical model. Moreover, he was a loyal partisan of the classics, he tells Chauvet, in holding that to combine tragedy and comedy 'destroys the unity of impression necessary for arousing emotion and sympathy. . . . But to forbid genius the use of the materials that are to be found in Nature, because it cannot produce good results from them, is obviously to push criticism beyond its purposes and its powers.' Shakespeare had seen the two elements combined in real life. He desired to reproduce the strong impression which the combination had made upon him and he was at perfect liberty to do so.

So far from being immoral, Shakespeare 'is superior to the others because he is more moral.'[2] And Manzoni's meaning is explained in the fragments of his proposed essay, *Della Moralità delle Opere Tragiche*.[3] The principal argument urged to prove that 'the drama is in its very essence immoral is that its aim is to excite the passions' by making us sympathize with the characters in all that they go through. This is true to a great extent of

---

[1] *Op. Ined.*, III. 176.   [2] *Ib.*, III. 163.   [3] *Ib.*, III.

I

French tragedy. But it is also possible to make the spectator 'stand aside from the characters and yet feel; to make him the judge. Notable example, Shakespeare.' The spectator feels due horror at the crimes of Richard III, Macbeth or Othello, yet cannot withhold his pity for their fate.

Manzoni's reminiscences and imitations of Shakespeare have been collected by Paolo Bellezza.[1] Manzoni himself freely admitted his indebtedness and pointed out the resemblance of the beautiful scene of Ermengarda's death, beginning 'Qui, sotto il tiglio qui' (*Adelchi*, iv), to the famous scene of Queen Katharine's death in *Henry VIII*, iii. 1, beginning, 'Take thy lute, wench,' which, as we have seen, had even been imitated by Alfieri.[2] We only propose to give a few noticeable instances, referring the reader to Bellezza's article for close verbal parallels. In *Carmagnola* a general resemblance has been traced between Othello's position and that of the great condottiere. Carmagnola's dignified bearing after his condemnation recalls that of Richard II and of Buckingham in *Henry VIII* in similar circumstances, the interview with his wife and daughter (v. 5) especially suggesting that between Richard and his Queen (v. 1). Again, the scenes between the commanders (ii. 1–3) are like those in 1 *Henry IV*, iv, 1 and 4. And it is worth remembering that the People appeared as a speaking character in the first draft of the play.

The following instance will show how Manzoni

[1] *Gli Studi Shakespeariani del Manzoni*, in *Giorn. Stor. Letter. Ital.* (1898), p. 251.

[2] S. Stampa, *Al. Manzoni, La sua Famiglia*, &c., I. 52–3.

could develop an idea which he had borrowed from Shakespeare :

> *Cassius.*   Come hither, sirrah :
> In Parthia did I take thee prisoner ;
> And then I swore thee, saving of thy life,
> That whatsoever I did bid thee do,
> Thou should'st attempt it. Come now, keep thine oath.
> —(*Julius Cæsar*, v. 3.)

> *Guntigi.* Amri, sovvienti di Spoleti ?
> *Amri.*   E posso
> Obliarlo, signor ?
> *Guntigi.*   D'allor che, morto
> Il tuo signor, solo, dai nostri cinto,
> Senza difesa rimanesti ? Alzata
> Sul tuo capo la scure, un furibondo
> Giù la calava ; io lo ritenni ; ai piedi
> Tu mi cadesti e ti gridasti mio.
> Che mi giuravi ?
> *Amri.*   Ubbidienza e fede,
> Fino alla morte.—O mio signor, falsato
> Ho il giuro mai ?
> *Guntigi.*   Non ; ma l'istante è giunto
> Che tu lo illustri con la prova.—(*Adelchi*, iv. 2.)

But Manzoni's indebtedness to Shakespeare went far deeper than this. 'Les manières et les allures du maître sont si bien reproduites qu'on imagine un moment l'entendre lui-même dans cette langue étrangère et plus harmonieuse,' says the *Revue Européenne* (15 May, 1861). The numerous soliloquies are obviously modelled on Shakespeare. Throughout the play Adelchi's dissatisfaction with the world as he finds it reminds one of

Hamlet, and the soliloquy 'Va, vivi, invecchia in pace' (v. 2), with its reflections on suicide, is clearly reminiscent of the same play, though Bellezza has pointed out the similarity of the opening words to

> Now the gods keep you old enough . . .—(*Timon*, iii. 6).

Guntigi's monologue (*Adelchi*, iv, 3) 'Fedeltà . . . ' reads like an amplification of Enobarbus's justification of his desertion of Antony :

> The loyalty well held to fools does make
> Our faith mere folly . . .—(*Antony and Cleopatra*, iii. 13).

Manzoni has even caught some of Shakespeare's tricks of style, such as his fondness for proverbial and general expressions. In fact, he has steeped himself in the English poet, or rather in Le Tourneur's translation, for he knew no English and even quotes the words from *Henry VIII*, given above, in French—'Prends ton luth'. We find him writing to Fauriel for a copy of Le Tourneur for a friend (23 May, 1817).

Shakespeare's influence upon Manzoni was at once recognized both at home and abroad. He 'has taken Shakespeare's historical plays for his models,' says *Blackwood* (Vol. II. p. 164). Ugo Foscolo, now an exile in London, wrote an article for the *Foreign Quarterly*, 'Della Nuova Scuola Drammatica Italiana.'[1] In this he points out the absurdity of Manzoni trying to preserve exact historical truth in tragedy and declares that Shakespeare himself could not make heroes out of English historical characters until his imagination had mended

[1] *Opere*, Vol. IV. p. 293.

them. In his greatest achievements, Hamlet, Othello and Macbeth, he was not hampered in this way and therefore he was successful. Madame de Stael had already expressed the same opinion in her *De la Littérature* (1808), Pt. I. chap. xiii, though she fully recognized the great popularity of the historical plays in England. Foscolo speaks enthusiastically of *Othello*, pointing out how Shakespeare transfers all our indignation at the Moor's crime to Iago, whom we cannot help admiring for his diabolical cunning. *The Tempest* shows Shakespeare's powers as a creator. Shakespeare 'copied whole pages of speeches and, without troubling to do more than put them into verse, assigned them to his characters. But this tragic poet rescued them from obscurity, breathed warmth and light into them, and added to them so skilfully that at every word they give us an insight into the human heart.'[1] It is, of course, impossible to say how much of this criticism of Shakespeare Foscolo owed to his English friends.

Nor did Manzoni's debt to Shakespeare end with his plays. In the *Promessi Sposi*, which has probably had more influence in Italy than any other novel in any other country, Padre Cristoforo possibly owes something to Friar Laurence, while resemblances have been traced between Gertrude's father and Capulet, and L'Innominato and Richard III. Here at last Manzoni could give full rein to the delightful humour which he had excluded so severely from his plays and which may well owe something to his Shakespeare studies. Moreover,

[1] *Opere*, IV. 319.

in Chapter iv he speaks of Banco's Ghost and in Chapter vii we read that 'between the first mention of a dreadful thing and the acting of it (said a barbarian not without ability) the interim is like a hideous dream, full of phantasms and terrors.' His attention may have been drawn to this passage by Monti, who, as we have seen, made use of it twice, or by Schlegel, who quotes it in Chapter xvii of his lectures on dramatic art, which were thoroughly familiar to Manzoni.

But the battle between Romanticism and Classicism was not yet over, and irony is a dangerous weapon at such times. Strange though it may seem to us now, Ignazio Valletta took the remark in all seriousness. 'I do not know', he says in the Preface to his translation of *Julius Cæsar* (1829), 'what a distinguished author can have meant when, after recently quoting a passage from *Julius Cæsar*, he begins his page "said a barbarian not without ability."' And he goes on to give vent to his indignation at Shakespeare, 'by whose name a nation swears as Jove swore by the waters of Styx', being called a barbarian. The first English translator of the *Promessi Sposi* (Rev. C. Swan) was so perturbed that he even wrote to expostulate with Manzoni on the subject. Manzoni answered that he felt like the man in the comedy (i.e., Beaumarchais's *Le Mariage de Figaro*) who enjoys being beaten by his jealous wife, because it is a proof of her love, 'on seeing you so angry with me in defence of my Shakespeare; for, though I do not understand a word of English and only know him in translations, I am so enthusiastic an admirer of him that it pains me to find others claiming to admire him more than myself.' And he proceeds to express his indignation at Voltaire's strictures.[1]

The controversy aroused by the Romantic Movement brings Shakespeare into prominence even in the anti-romantic reviews like the *Biblioteca Italiana* and the *Spettatore*, though the *Accattabrighe, ossia Classico-Roman-ticomachia* (November, 1818–March, 1819), which was started in direct opposition to the *Conciliatore*, barely mentions him in a dialogue on the unities. The two former naturally speak favourably of Carlo Londonio's *Cenni Critici sulla Poesia Romantica* (1817). In an article on Torti's *Sulla Poesia* and Ermes Visconti's *Idee Elementari sulla Poesia Romantica*, which is a reprint of his articles in the *Conciliatore*, the *Biblioteca Italiana* (Febuary, 1819) says that a tragedy ought to be serious and dignified thoughout. 'Shakespeare, who is always on the lips of the Romantics, Shakespeare, whose example could never prove anything, because there is no evidence that his tragedies would please Italians, Shakespeare, who could not obey the rules, which he had not learnt owing to his lack of education, Shake-speare made that mistake in all his tragedies. Falstaff, so popular in England, would certainly be ridiculed in an Italian tragedy and the author held up to scorn. . . . Even the highest people forget their dignity.' And he quotes instances from *Antony and Cleopatra*. 'These vulgarities destroy that *unity of the heart*, which cannot but be divided between the misfortunes of the

[1] See *The Betrothed Lovers* (1828).

heroes, which move us to pity, and their coarse vices and trivial talk, which call forth our contempt and laughter.' The criticism is, of course, still largely Voltaire's.

In this very year, however, the *Spettatore*, Vol. X. pp. 659–60 contains the advertisement of Michele Leoni's proposed translation of Shakespeare to be completed in two years, if two hundred and fifty subscribers are forthcoming. The *Tragedie di Shakspeare, Tradotte da Michele Leoni,* appeared in fourteen volumes between 1819 and 1822, dedicated to Ferdinand I, King of the Two Sicilies (Verona, dalla Società Tipografica). Each play was preceded by Schlegel's Introduction and provided with copious notes by the translator, while the first volume contained a version of Johnson's *Essay on Shakespeare* and Rowe's *Life. The Tempest, King John, Midsummer Night's Dream, Othello, Macbeth, Julius Cæsar, Romeo and Juliet, Richard III, Cymbeline* and *Hamlet* were revisions of earlier translations, both prose and verse being done into blank verse. Leoni adopted this plan, he tells us, because Shakespeare often puts his most poetical ideas into prose, and because a mixture of prose and verse would sound strange in Italian ears. *King Lear, Richard II* and the two parts of *Henry IV* were in prose, not only because prose admitted of greater accuracy, but also because Leoni considered that he had already translated the most poetical plays and found that English historical names were unmanageable in Italian verse.

The translation is not very satisfactory, as one would expect from the quantity of work produced by this

'Translator Generale', to give him Philemon Holland's title. It is often very free. This is the rendering of the opening of Brutus's speech in *Julius Cæsar*, 'Be patient till the last. Romans, countrymen and lovers!'

> Sino al fin del sermon chiuso rimanga
> Il labbro vostro, o amici, onde non suoni
> Parola indarno. Quel che dir mi appresto
> Sia creduto da voi pel mio decoro:
> Ne al mio decoro di credenza ingrati
> Siate così, che il raggionar sia vano.

The prose versions are, of course, more accurate, but *Henry IV* is frequently bowdlerized, Leoni generally following Le Tourneur in his omissions. In his *Lettera Semiseria di Grisostomo*, which was the real manifesto of Romanticism in Italy (1816), Giovanni Berchet says that Leoni would have been an ideal translator of Shakespeare, if he had chosen prose for his medium. 'His verses are good Italian verses, but . . . Shakespeare is lost sight of and we are obliged to envy the French their Le Tourneur.' There is more than a grain of truth in this criticism.

The publishers tell us in a prefatory note that when these versions began to appear they were not as successful as they deserved to be. A number of people, 'alarmed at the idea that the genius of the Italian Parnassus was likely to suffer serious injury by the issue of works of this kind, were led to boycott them incontinently from a misunderstood feeling of national pride; while others, possessed of rather more sense, would only approve of a few passages. But as neither class could help being affected by the strong emotions by which that all-powerful writer so often proves that an opinion is wrong, or revenges himself for an ill-considered dislike, the tragedies were read and re-read' and were now out of print. Leoni himself calls Shakespeare the Michelangelo of tragedy and, like a true son of the didactic eighteenth century, he is careful to point out the good which may be derived from them. 'There is now no one who does not think that from the works of this rarest of geniuses are to be drawn lessons concerning the most important circumstances of life and metaphysical doctrines that could be adopted with profit and honour in the literature of our country.' There is probably no poet, with the exception of Dante and Alfieri, in whom philosophy does so much to make his readers think.

But by the time Manzoni's tragedies and Leoni's translations had appeared the battle was really won. Critics might approve of Shakespeare's methods or not, but the Romantic movement had at least made it impossible for them to ignore him or treat him with contempt. He was universally recognized as one of the world's great poets with whose works every cultivated person should be acquainted. 'Italians and foreigners, drawn by a feeling of piety,' says the *Antologia* (December, 1824), 'visit the tomb of the two hapless lovers in Verona, whose story, after being made known to the world by our own writers, furnished Shakespeare with the subject for his moving tragedy.' Shakespeare's position was indeed assured when Verona had thus become a place of pilgrimage for Italians as well as for Englishmen on his account.

Gherardini, the translator of Schlegel's *Lectures*, who was, as we have seen, no sympathizer with the new movement, says, in his *Elementi di Poesia ad uso delle Scuole* (1820), that Shakespeare's 'sovereign genius' understood how to introduce 'with such skill and in so novel a way a soliloquy of such a nature that it produced the most stupendous, the most terrible scene that has ever been written.' Then follows a description of the sleep-walking scene in *Macbeth* (p. 330). Elsewhere he ascribes Shakespeare's popularity, in spite of his defects, to his use of the marvellous (p. 316). Neither of these criticisms is, of course, original.

The change of tone in the reviews is most marked. In the *Biblioteca Italiana* for October, 1821 there is a long article on Leoni's Shakespeare and, after discounting all that the writer acknowledges that he has taken from Johnson's *Essay*, his criticisms are of real interest. To judge such a poet by Aristotle's rules is as absurd as to try a Republican by the laws of monarchy, he declares, clearly borrowing the idea from a remark in Pope's *Essay*. We must not let our classical prejudices prevent us from recognizing the qualities in which he is superior. The fact that a cultivated people has so long felt for him a 'reverence amounting to superstition' is proof positive of his greatness. Then follow a number of criticisms taken almost entirely from Johnson. Shakespeare is the poet of nature, who sets before us a faithful picture of life. His characters are not individuals, they are species.

His plays are neither tragedies nor comedies, but show us life in all its aspects. His comic scenes are clearly more natural and spontaneous than his tragic ; and there are other judgments from the same source. The writer follows Johnson in his opinion that the ends of the plays are less carefully finished than the beginnings. Shakespeare seems to become indifferent when the goal is in sight. A summary of Johnson's arguments in defence of Shakespeare's violation of the rules is given, nor is any attempt made to reply to them. The reviewer does not share the view that Leoni ought to have used prose for his translations, though he thinks that much of Shakespeare's poetry would sound strange in Italian verse :—'All the world's a stage', for instance. Then he quotes Act I of *Julius Cæsar* and points out how magnificently vigorous it is and yet how little it obeys the ordinary rules of rhetoric. Who would venture to assert that Aristotle's canons would have been the same if he had had Shakespeare instead of the Greek tragic poets before him ? After all, the rules were only derived from the tragedians. This is indeed an admission from the *Biblioteca Italiana*.

There is probably not a single Italian reader, proceeds the reviewer, who is not familiar with *Othello*, or at least with the tragic story upon which it is founded. ' It is considered to be Shakespeare's best stage play. . . . After *Othello* comes *Macbeth* ; and this is the tragedy which seems to be usually preferred by the English as most calculated to make one think. On our stage the scenes with the witches, especially the scene that takes place in their cave while they are uttering their spells over their boiling magic cauldron, would not only be repulsive, but altogether insufferable.' There is hardly a page in the play that does not make one shudder. Macbeth and Lady Macbeth are drawn with 'stupendous truth'. As for Leoni's translation, some people would find his verse 'too splendid to be tragic'. But the criticism would probably not displease him and in any case Alfieri's style would be quite out of place for Juliet, Desdemona or Miranda; and it is in dealing with the feelings and in the art of leading up to them that Shakespeare is superior to everyone else. Those ignorant of English need no longer turn to 'Le Tourneur's feeble, not to say altogether lifeless versions'.

In an article on Manzoni's *Adelchi* (1824) we read that 'our Alfieri has certainly reached the highest point in his art, but as he was nearly always concerned with political questions and handled strong emotions such as are experienced by but few people, he will never obtain in Italy the wide fame and the almost divine honours which in England are bestowed upon the author of *Othello*.' *Othello* already seems to be superseding *Romeo and Juliet* in general favour in Italy, where it is still perhaps the most frequently acted of Shakespeare's plays. In 1826 (Vol. I. p. 63) we are told that Shakespeare, 'the favourite model of the Romantics,' is, for all his coarseness, distinguished by beauty and originality more easy to admire than to imitate; and, moreover, he is not romantic, but classic. Unfortunately the writer does not explain his meaning.

But Voltaire's view was not by any means dead. As

late as 1831 Antonio Riccardi reproduced it almost
undiluted in his *Manuale di Ogni Letteratura*, where
Shakespeare is credited with being the author of music-
dramas in the same fantastic and extravagant style as his
tragedies and comedies. Still more astonishing does
Riccardi find it that a certain sect called Romantics holds
him up 'as the universal patriarch of the theatre of every
nation' (pp. 393-4). Similarly, Count Giambattista
Carrara-Spinelli of Bergamo gives expression to his indignation at the craze for English literature in his Epistle to
Giuseppe Pallavicini, *Sulla Smania delle Donne per la
Moderna Letteratura* and his ode *Sulla Soverchia Imitazione
degli Inglesi*. Though he can find much to admire in
Shakespeare, he is even more explicit in his Epistle to·
Cav. Ippolito Pindemonte *Sulla Poesia Romantica*, which
invokes

> Dal Sire
> De'Bardi Ossian la pace, e dal tremendo
> Britanno Sakespir . . .
> Quindi muggir, come il Gargano, udresti
> I Lombardi teatri, ove alle scene
> Merope tornì : a spalancata bocca
> Desdemona, Desdemona gridando
> Stuol novator di vati il circo assorda . . .
> Piace un Moro feroce, ed istrumento
> Fatto di strana morte un origliere.
> È ver che tra plebeo sermon non rado
> Splendon carmi divini, o sovra l'ale
> Amlet s'innalzi di sublime sogno,
> O segga l'improvvisa ombra di Banco
> A fronte di Macbet.

In any case, all but common minds detest imitation. 'Costoro,' he asks

Forse di Sakespir ebber l'ingegno?[1]

Nor does Antonio Beduschi, in his *Sullo Stato Attuale della Tragedia in Italia* (1827), consider that Shakespeare is a good model for modern Italy, since the character of her literature has always been diametrically opposed to that of the English and Germans (p. 11). Following Sismondi, he holds that in *Saul* Alfieri has drawn closer to the *idoleggiato Shakespeare* (p. 43), and, like Madame de Stael and Foscolo, he believes that it is in drawing ideal characters and not in handling historical facts that Shakespeare is most successful. His plays were 'imagined by that gigantic intellect in the spirit of his own times', but the delicate taste of the modern world would find it impossible to tolerate his horrors. Moreover, an age which concedes so little to the imagination would equally dislike the style of his 'diabolical and cabalistic poetry . . . and the mixture of tears and laughter, prose and verse' (p. 101).

The last serious attempt to defend the crumbling ruins of the old fortress was, however, made by Count G. U. Pagani-Cesa in his *Sovra Il Teatro Tragico Italiano* (1825). In Shakespeare 'princes and plebeians, the serious and the comic, verse and prose' are jumbled together, as we have so often been told before. 'I will only observe that Milton, steeped though he is in the beauties of Shakespeare, finds in him the roughness of

---

[1] Carrara-Spinelli, *Versi e Prose* (1827).

the times in which he wrote; that Pope affirms that
Shakespeare wrote both better and worse than anybody
else; and that Addisson wrote his *Cato*, a masterpiece
applauded by all nations, in accordance with the rules,
which seem unassailable and which lie at the foundation
of the classic theatre. These three names carry far more
weight than a licence which is not only tolerated, but
welcomed in a country where the people stand on a
footing of equality with persons of position' (p. 9).
French and Italian critics have long admired all that
deserves admiration in Shakespeare without approving
of his extravagances and improbabilities (p. 93). England stands alone in her constitution and her history
and Shakespeare suits her. The People rule England
and should therefore have a place in her theatre, but
this is not the case elsewhere (p. 97). And in the
course of the dialogue between the Englishman and the
Italian (p. 82), the Italian says that 'the romantic style
will never be anything but monstrous: and if it is to
be tolerated, there will always have to be a Shakespear,
whom the romantic, but not wildly romantic England
does not promise to produce again; and if this Shakespear is to be received with equal honour outside
England, the world will have to become altogether
English in politics and character, a state of affairs which
is not likely to come about.' The idea of deriving one
of the distinctive features of Elizabethan drama from
our democratic constitution is interesting.

But the importance of Pagani-Cesa's book lies in the
criticisms to which it gave rise. The Count was an old

man and Bertolotti declared in the *Nuovo Ricoglitore* (11 November, 1825) that he 'belongs to another epoch of our literature. He is a kind of poetic shade returning from the Elysian Fields or, better still, a sleeper awakening once again after long years of sleep, real or apparent.' Though he finds much to commend in the book when it deals with Italian tragedy of the past, he prophesies that 'it will not probably be well treated in other papers.' Nor was he mistaken. The *Biblioteca Italiana* (1827), Vol. XLVI. p. 6, refuses to believe that the English poets mentioned by Pagani-Cesa did not share the general opinion concerning Shakespeare. Milton calls him 'amabile figlio della fantasia'—'sweetest Shakespeare, Fancy's child'—a quotation which the reviewer is more likely to have taken from Schlegel's *Lectures* (chap. xxii), than from Meneghelli's *Dissertazione sopra la Tragedia Cittadinesca*—and we must not attach too much importance to his remarks in his political pamphlets.[1] In Pope's day Shakespeare's imitators had brought him into disrepute by imitating his defects rather than his good qualities. Pope saw his faults, but he admired his greatness and therefore edited him.

---

[1] The reviewer, like Count Pagani-Cesa, is probably referring to the passage in Section 1 of *Eikonoklastes*, where Milton talks of instancing not an abstruse author, but one 'whom we well know was the closest companion of these his [i. e., the King's] solitudes, William Shakespeare' as introducing Richard III 'speaking in as high a strain of piety and mortification as any in this book.' He quotes Act ii. 1:

> 'I do not know that Englishman alive
> With whom my soul is any jot at odds
> More than the infant that is born to-night;
> I thank my God for my humility,'

and remarks that 'other stuff of this sort may be read throughout the whole tragedy'. Milton, however, is not here criticizing Shakespeare as a poet, but attacking the sentiments he has put into the mouth of a tyrant like Richard III.

K

Whatever merits Addison's *Cato* may possess, 'the distance which separates it from *Othello* is boundless.' If Pagani-Cesa does not realize this, we may discuss history and politics with him, but not poetry.

The liberal and romantic *Antologia* makes the book a pretext for proclaiming its adherence to the new dramatic school in three elaborate articles by Montani (Feb., March and April, 1826). Voltaire is to blame if Italians can only picture Shakespeare 'surrounded by ghosts and tortures, daggers and poisons ; always ready to plunge our imaginations into terror or gloom by all that is most horrible in crime or most degrading in vice.' Most of the current criticism is still based upon Voltaire. The writer quotes the *Mercurio del Secolo XIX* to the effect that Shakespeare is the most moral of authors, since he enables us to pity Macbeth or Othello, for all our hatred of their crimes. And how tender he can be! Italians should least of all be led astray by Voltaire, since he treated Dante in exactly the same manner. How is it that the critics who attack Shakespeare for his coarseness have nothing to say against Aristophanes on that score? In Shakespeare's day, too, women did not act, nor did they often go to the theatre ; and we all know that 'men make laws, women make manners'. The writer frequently quotes Schlegel. Could anything, he goes on to ask, be more ridiculous than to exclude the People from tragedy (on the ground that they take no part in government) after the French Revolution? 'Those most opposed to his methods, unless they refuse altogether to listen to reason and truth, are now agreed in saying that no one understands better than he how to set a picture of human life before the spectator's eyes, no one has traced more successfully than he the course of the passions that tyrannise over man and his fate, no one has more unerringly divined their language, no one has created dramatic situations better fitted to bring them out. Everyone is agreed in recognising that he possesses an inexhaustible source of invention, and a kind of creative force that gives life to countless beings, each one so real and yet so different.' Moreover, competent judges praise his style highly. The other articles prove that romantic plays are not mere monstrosities and attack the absurd conventions of the unities, which indeed had almost ceased to be worth attacking. To some of these criticisms Pagani-Cesa replied in an appendix to a reprint of his book, but the *Biblioteca Italiana* was deemed worthy of a special pamphlet from his pen, the *Mazzo di Fiori*.

In the *Antologia* for April 1826 is a letter from Carlo Botta in answer to one from Luigi de Brême, written from Coppet, the headquarters of the heresy, where he was Madame de Stael's guest. He sighs to see his wretched country running after *tedescherie* as soon as it has grown tired of *franceserie*. He fully admits Shakespeare's greatness. 'Yet he would be a greater poet, had he not mixed the heroic with the vulgar. So would Schiller, only Schiller does deliberately what Shakespeare did from ignorance.' Botta speaks in much the same way of Dante, blaming him for his abstruseness. But he was fighting for a lost cause. And in 1828 it was even thought worth while to publish an Italian version of Mrs. Montagu's *Essay* in Florence.

Then, in 1830, Mazzini contributed his three articles *Del Dramma Storico*, as well as his *Della Fatalità considerata com' Elemento Drammatico* to the *Antologia*. They long had a very powerful influence on Italian opinion. To Mazzini Shakespeare is the great individualist, in whom we find the highest expression of the *ego*, without the conception of collectivity. He does not call up his characters, he creates them. 'Shakespear's men possess life and movement as if they came from the hand of God; a life one, and varied, and harmonious.' Dumas called Shakespeare the greatest creator after God, but the God-fearing Pellico went one better in a letter of 1833 to Santa Rosa, when he probably had this article by Mazzini in mind. God is various, he says, because he is infinite 'and because he can (like that Shakespeare of Shakespeares that he is) employ variety with a master hand to produce a wise unity.'

Though Shakespeare's characters are governed by necessity, says Mazzini, they have their fate in their own hands, but the passions are the instruments which make it impossible for them to escape its grasp. Dante, Tacitus and Michelangelo alone possess some of Shakespeare's marvellous power of hitting off a character in a few strokes. By pure creative power he produced a Hamlet two centuries before he could possibly be understood. Mazzini, however, regarded literature as a means to something greater and more important than itself. And Shakespeare's genius merely summed up, it did not create ; it reproduced a past epoch, it did not proclaim a new one. Shakespeare had no great guiding moral principle. He was no prophet and there is a despairing bitterness in his reflections on the vanity of life, a cynicism that is only another side of his individualism. He lacked all those qualities which appealed irresistibly to Mazzini in Dante and, in a lesser degree, in Byron. Mazzini gives the difference between Shakespeare's outlook, as he conceives it, and his own in a letter to Mrs. Peter Taylor (9 March, 1857).[1]

When Shakespeare criticism has reached this stage in Italy we may safely leave it. But as an answer to Mazzini we may quote the following words of Francesco de Sanctis, the greatest Italian literary critic of the last century, though they were not written till 1869–70.[2] He is talking of Dante's *Inferno*. 'Those mighty figures, stiff and epic as statues there upon their pedestals, are awaiting the artist who shall take them by the hand and cast them into the whirlpool of life and make them dramatic. And the artist was not an Italian : he was Shakespeare.'

[1] B. King, *Mazzini*, p. 357.   [2] *Storia della Lett. Ital.*, I. p. 200.

VIII

SHAKESPEARE's triumph, which was due to the Romantic Movement, may be said to have culminated in the appearance of no fewer than four translations between 1830 and 1831. Giuseppe Niccolini's *Macbet* was published at Brescia in 1830. The others all appeared in Milan which was then, as now, the centre of the book trade in Italy. In the following year Gaetano Barbieri, a Professor of Mathematics, brought out a *Romeo and Juliet* there, also in verse. Not only had he translated Alfred de Vigny's *More de Venise*, but he left a verse translation of *Othello* behind him at his death. Then three volumes of a translation by Giunio Bazzoni and Giacomo Sornani, the lyrics only being in verse, which included *Othello, Tempest, King Lear, Macbeth, Midsummer Night's Dream* and *Romeo and Juliet*, were printed in 1830–1, and prose translations of *Othello* and *Macbeth* by Virginio Soncini in 1830. The *Antologia* (June, 1831) considers Barbieri's *Romeo and Juliet* more accurate, if less vigorous than Leoni's. But Niccolini's *Macbet* was by far the best of these efforts. Battaglia, in a paper on Italian translators of Shakespeare,[1] quotes his rendering of the scene of Banquo's murder as a model of the way in which Italian verse should be used in the drama. In

[1] *Mosaico*, p. 107.

addition to these, which were reviewed at length by Francesco Ambrosoli in the *Biblioteca Italiana* (January, 1831), Ignazio Valletta published prose versions of *Julius Cæsar* (1829), *Othello* (1830) and *Coriolanus* (1834) at Florence.

In the February number of the *Biblioteca Italiana* for 1831 Ambrosoli seeks an explanation for the fact that not one of these translations had proved successful enough to induce its author to continue it. A few years ago, he says, the battle over the unities was at its height, though no one would now trouble to open his mouth on the subject. It is true that the old theories still possess a few supporters, but the number of those who have embraced the new faith, at least so far as no longer to consider a man a barbarian if he does not obey the rules, is very great. He finds the explanation in the fact that the playwright must be national to be popular and this Shakespeare can never be in Italy. And he, too, follows Mazzini in holding that Shakespeare has no message of hope to give, since his world is ruled by chance.

But surely we need not go so far afield for the explanation. Translations, especially of poetry, are rarely very successful. Moreover, as Ambrosoli saw, there was an unusual demand for a translation of Shakespeare at the height of the romantic controversy, when everyone was talking about him. This was supplied by Leoni, or even by Le Tourneur, since all cultivated Italians can read French. Nor was Leoni's version likely to be dethroned from its position except by one that was either more complete or greatly superior. But of the translations mentioned Niccolini's *Macbet* alone was distinctly better than Leoni's, while none of them was so complete.

When Carlo Rusconi published his complete prose translation of the plays in two volumes with continuous pagination at Padua in 1839 it supplied a want and, though Battaglia complains that he could find no reference to it in the reviews, it soon became known, and has been reprinted many times. It is far more accurate than Leoni's and often really good. The translation of *Hamlet* is still the standard one in Italy on the stage and elsewhere. In the same year Professor Jean, of Parma, brought out a blank verse rendering of the *Merchant of Venice*, which Battaglia considered too faithful to the English to be really Italian, and sent round proposals for a new complete translation; but it is hardly surprising to learn that they were not taken up.

Giulio Carcano's translation has, however, now become the standard work in Italy. At the age of twenty-seven, in 1839, he published versions of some scenes from *King Lear*, and thenceforth, we are told,[1] his translation of Shakespeare became at once the torment and the delight of his life. In 1843 appeared his *Teatro Scelto di Shakespeare* (Milano, Pirola), and in 1857 another edition in three volumes (Firenze, Le Monnier), containing *Lear, Hamlet, Julius Cæsar, Romeo and Juliet, Macbeth, Richard III, Othello, Tempest, Merchant of Venice* and *Henry VIII.* The plays were nearly all published separately as well.

[1] See the Memoir in Vol. I of his *Opere Complete* (1892).

[*To face p.* 137.

GIULIO CARCANO.
(From the bust outside the door of the Brera Library, Milan.)

Then between 1875 and 1882 the complete edition in twelve volumes was published by Hoepli in Milan. Carcano was busy revising his work during his whole life and it was only completed two years before his death. His bust now stands just outside the door of the Brera Library in Milan.

Carcano's translation deserves the position it holds in general estimation. He was an ardent disciple of Manzoni and his blank verse owes not a little to his master. Not only is he far more accurate than Leoni, but his lines often catch something of a Shakespearean ring, especially in the more rhetorical and poetical passages—in the Queen Mab speech, for instance. And he is at great pains in choosing his Italian equivalents —e.g., his rendering of

> If it were done when 'tis done, then 'twere well
> It were done quickly

by the Italian proverb,

> Se capo ha cosa fatta, è meglio assai
> Che subito sia fatto.

There have, of course, been numerous translations of single plays published during the last half century. Quite recently Signor Diego Angeli, encouraged by the success of his version of the *Midsummer Night's Dream* for Arthur Rackham's illustrations, and considering that Italians 'have never had the hardihood to reproduce the simplicity and often the roughness of Shakespeare', has embarked upon an entirely new translation, which Hoepli is publishing in Milan. In the Introduction to the *Tempest*, the first volume (1911), he tells us how 'the almost religious feeling I have always had for the great English poet' dates from his early boyhood, when he used to turn over the pages of an illustrated English Shakespeare during the quiet of the midday summer siesta in an old Tuscan villa, till he learnt to know and to love the characters. It was Titania, however, who above all attracted his childish fancy and he used to look anxiously under the flowers in the hope of getting a glimpse of the fairies and their queen during his walks. The *Midsummer Night's Dream* is the only one of the comedies that has been generally appreciated in Latin countries, where the tragedies have always been most popular and best understood. Its early appeal to Signor Angeli only proves how well fitted he is by temperament for the task he has undertaken.

IX

SHAKESPEARE AND THE LATER ROMANTIC DRAMA
IN ITALY

WHEN we turn to the playwrights, we find that Manzoni
has definitely fixed the length to which it was possible
to carry romantic theories in the drama in Italy, and
his followers, to quote Bertana (*La Tragedia*, p. 375),
generally remain on the hither side of the line he has
drawn. As a playwright Victor Hugo had very little
influence in the peninsula where, after 1830, the very
word romantic fell into evil repute. Classical tradition
was never completely in abeyance south of the Alps,
where the triumph of undiluted romanticism would be
an impossibility. Carlo Tedaldi-Fores expresses the
feelings of his brother dramatists in his *Epistola a Cesare
Arici* (1822):

> L'angla letteratura e la tedesca
> S'abbia in pregio ad ognor, nonchè l'austera
> E delicata simmetria francesca ;
> Ma per questo non fia che la maniera
> Diserti, onde fu grande il buon Virgilio,
> Petrarca, Dante e gli altri di lor schiera.
> Di Sciller e di Scêchspir diletto piglio,
> Ma non così ch' io n'abbia ad obliare
> D'essere di questa umile Italia figlio.

Moreover, in accordance with Manzoni's example, these
tragedies were invariably historical and were provided

with elaborate historical introductions. Subjects were generally taken from the past history of Italy, more especially from the mediæval period, with the object of arousing patriotic enthusiasm in the country. The writers were themselves patriots almost to a man and their work had a deliberate purpose. Traces of Shakespeare's influence are neither so numerous, nor so obvious as before. He was so well known that it was no longer possible to borrow from him quite so openly.

Now that Manzoni had shown the way a definite type of romantic tragedy was rapidly developed from which the variations were slight. The scene was frequently changed and the unity of time was no longer regarded as binding, but the latitude allowed himself by Manzoni in *Carmagnola* was seldom imitated. In structure these plays differed, of course, but little from the classical model. Nor was the comic element introduced into tragedy. As Carlo Marenco put it, the two schools, each of which was defective when pushed to extremes, had now found neutral ground where they could shake hands. In fact, Shakespeare's influence was exercised rather through Manzoni, or even through Goethe and Schiller, than directly. Thus in the Introduction to his *I Fieschi e I Doria* (1829), though Tedaldi-Fores declares that no one understands how to reproduce the past better than Shakespeare and even speaks of him with enthusiasm, he is obviously more familiar with Schiller, mentioning several of his plays by name and telling us that he has been careful to read *William Tell*, probably in Maffei's translation, in order to avoid imitating it in his own tragedy. The object of these writers was to create a modern national theatre and 'since Shakespear's genius seemed at times to elude these aims of theirs by its very vastness and the infinite variety of its forms, they turned with greater confidence to Schiller who, as they believed, had been guided by the same national purpose and the same needs.'[1]   Hence after 1830 we have not attempted to make an exhaustive examination of the works of the numerous writers whom Manzoni's example encouraged to produce poor tragedies in verse, but have confined our attention to two or three of the best of them.

G. B. de Cristoforis was the one notable exception who ventured to go beyond Manzoni. His *Sergianni Caracciolo* (1826) does not rise above the average of plays of this kind, and though the story of Queen Giovanna's all-powerful minister owes much to *Carmagnola*, the author is obviously familiar with both Shakespeare and Schiller. The council held by the Queen at the end of the first act is distinctly Shakespearean in tone, especially the Queen's speech to the Papal Legate. So are the description of the courage of Gennaro's father, followed by Sergianni's making Gennaro his page, and the soliloquies and the frequent gnomic sentences. More remarkable, however, is de Cristoforis's daring in flying in the face of public opinion by introducing a comic element. The prisoner who is brought in for shouting 'Viva il triumvirato!' after the regatta (iii. 8) is imitated from Schiller's *Fiesco*, while the drunken soldiers

[1] Mazzucchetti, *Schiller in Italia*, p. 119.

in Act v are borrowed from Shakespeare. On these two scenes, 'for which Shakespeare's example will not, we imagine, be quoted,' the *Biblioteca Italiana* (Vol. XLIII) is particularly severe. 'We do not know from whence the defence of a device so strange will be forthcoming.' And Beduschi[1] speaks of him as the first to embellish Italian tragedy 'with the noble characters of a *lazzarone* and a drunken man talking the dialect of the scum of Naples. . . . These indecencies, these ravings' must not plead the excuse of a mind as divine as Shakespeare's. Nor do we think that anyone will claim that de Cristoforis has succeded in his attempt. But *Sergianni* stands alone.

To the same year (1826) belongs the *Giulietta e Romeo* of Cesare della Valle, Duca di Ventignano. It is the best of the Italian adaptations and follows Shakespeare fairly closely. Salvini appeared in it and it inspired Bellini's *Capuletti e Montecchi*. But it is a sad travesty of the original. The Finale is worth quoting. The scene is, of course, the Capulets' tomb.

Scena Ultima.

Capuleto, Lorenzo, Paride, Enrico, domestici con faci.

(Grido universale di dolore. Cade la tela.)

Silvio Pellico was, as we have seen, the first of the romantic dramatists. Of his *Francesca da Rimini* we have already spoken. In his best play, *Eufemio da Messina* (1820), we can find no special trace of Shakespeare. The scene of *Ester d'Engaddi* (1820–4), written during his imprisonment in Venice, which is laid outside the Jewish camp, is thoroughly romantic. In Azaria, the jealous,

[1] *Sullo Stato Attuale*, &c., p. 86.

impetuous husband who is instantly convinced of his wife's guilt by the lies of his trusted friend Jefte, the High Priest, we can hardly be wrong in seeing a reminiscence of Othello. Jefte, however, in no way recalls Iago. Iginia is tortured by the usual 'Shakespearean' visions in *Iginia d'Asti* (1821):

> No: assiso
> Vi sta uno spettro. Ahi vista! in volto scritto
> In note atre di sangue ha . . . 'il parricida' . . .
> Deh, come piange . . .—(iv. 2).

But, as we have seen, this kind of thing has become too common to be worth special attention.

Pellico's other tragedies are not of a high order, but it would be unfair to judge them harshly, considering the circumstances in which they were written. In *Boezio*, however, a posthumous tragedy, published for the first time by Rinieri, he draws much closer to Shakespeare, or rather to Manzoni, whose influence he would probably have felt to a far greater degree but for his long imprisonment in the Spielberg. Here the People plays an important part and the rich mingle with the poor, while the scene is frequently changed. But for the soliloquies and the comforting vision that appears to Boezio in the fifth act there is no need to look further than Manzoni. Otherwise we can find no certain traces of Shakespeare's influence, and Pellico's letter to Carlo Marenco (3 June, 1844)[1] proves that he was well aware of the difficulty of following Shakespeare's methods under modern theatrical conditions.

[1] *Epistolario*, p. 290.

Carlo Marenco, on the the other hand, was a loyal follower of Manzoni. His plays are accompanied by the elaborate historical introductions and notes of the time and are often divided into days instead of acts, though he shows more respect for the unities than his master. His *Pia dei Tolomei* was by far the most popular romantic tragedy of the day. It is a resetting of the story of *Othello*. Pia rejects the love of Ugo, who makes her husband think her unfaithful by letting him see her at night in conversation with a warrior disguised as her brother, who, unknown to her, has been killed in battle. Rinaldo, however, has none of Othello's impetuous energy, nor has Ugo anything of Iago's diabolical cunning, while Pia is a languishing and lacrimose sister of Ermengarda or Lucia in the *Promessi Sposi*. Yet Marenco has apparently been reading *Othello*.

> Sacro all' immagin tua mi fei nell' alma
> Segreto un tempio,—(iii. 1)

is surely an echo of 'But there where I have garner'd up my heart' (iv. 2), and Rinaldo's speech,

> Han veramente
> Quel ch' io a te mal credea, l'han veramente,
> Questi occhi scorto, e queste orecchie udito. . .—(ii. 5.)

reminds one in a general way of Othello's doubts (iii. 3). Similarly, the scene in which Rinaldo leaves Pia in a fury before sending her to the malaria-stricken castle where she is to die in a highly edifying manner, just when Ugo has confessed his guilt and Rinaldo has come to ask her forgiveness, suggests something of Othello before he strangles Desdemona. Ugo's repentance and confession, on the other hand, recall those of Iachimo in *Cymbeline*, but the resemblance may well be fortuitous.

Bondelmonte, Amedei and his sister in *Bondelmonte e gli Amedei* stand in much the same relation to each other as Hamlet, Laertes and Ophelia. The resemblance is, however, quite general and the heroine's languishing death, with chorus, harks back to *Adelchi*. The citizens, each of whom expresses his opinion at her funeral, are ultimately Shakespearean. So are the crowds in *Corso Donati* (1830), where Shakespeare's influence is not otherwise apparent. Again, in *Ezzelino Terzo* (1832) Mabilia's anxious following of her husband may owe something to *Coriolanus* or *Julius Cæsar*, though the resemblance is hardly worth pressing.

It is in *Ugolino*, however, that Marenco is most obviously imitating Shakespeare. Ugolino is entering Pisa in triumph (i. 10), when the exclamation,

> Nulla, Ugolin, ti manca
> Fuorche l'ira di Dio,

affects him exactly as Banquo's Ghost affects Macbeth. His sons and his daughter-in-law try to calm him, like Lady Macbeth. Ugolino's reply,

> Ah, se un core innocente, un' alma avessi
> Pura come la tua, dritta all' Eterno,
> E confidente, voleria dal petto
> D'Ugolin la preghiera. Ahimè! Dal peso
> Di colpe antiche, e di profan desiri
> Impedito il mio cor, vorrebbe indarno
> Ergersi infino a Dio,

L

is clearly a reminiscence of the King's soliloquy in *Hamlet*, 'O, my offence is rank' (iii. 3). Ruggieri's soliloquy (ii. 9) is also modelled on those of Shakespeare. Ugolino at bay recalls Richard III, and his exclamation,

> Oh rabbia ! Olà un destriere,'—(iv. 6)

was doubtless suggested by, 'A horse, a horse! My kingdom for a horse.'

Marenco seems to have been reading *Macbeth* while he was writing *Berengario Augusto* (1840). There is a general resemblance in the subject and Berengario's vision of his descendents (Act iv) reminds one of Banquo's. Moreover,

> Contra mortal qual sia difender oso
> La donna del mio cor.—(ii. 5)

is surely a reminiscence of

> I dare do all that may become a man ;
> Who dares do more is none.—(i. 7.)

Further, does not

> Un re non fugge. Ei mostra
> Impertubata ai traditor la fronte.
> Non s'asconde vilmente,—(Act v)

suggest Macbeth or Richard III? Again, in *Cecilia da Baone*, a posthumous tragedy, Gerardo's words,

> Le mie dure fatiche, i lunghi errori
> Narrarle mi parea, vederla pendere
> Da questo labbro, e sull' intento volto
> Notar le tumultuose ansie del cor,—(i. 3)

recall Othello's account of his wooing of Desdemona (iii. 1).

Carlo Tedaldi-Fores, a writer of even poorer historical plays which were never acted, says in the Introduction to his *I Fieschi e i Doria* (1829), to which we have already referred, that 'no one knew better than Shakespeare how to project himself into the past, adapt himself to all subjects, obtain a thorough grasp of the natures of historical characters and set them before us in contrast with the manners and customs of the age. Yet he did not copy history, but entered into a generous rivalry with it and turned it into poetry, often giving the rein to his own imagination and colouring the prose of life with its charm.' Still, as we have said, he was better acquainted with Schiller. The play contains an enormous number of characters and the scene is changed sixteen times, but the only possible Shakespearean reminiscence appears to be :

> Dell' arpa tua la voce in sul mio ciglio
> Stese il sonno e l'oblio. . . . Soave sonno
> Il piacere e il dolor sperdi e confondi
> Nell' ombra tua.—(iv. 16.)

This may be compared with the various passages in praise of sleep to be found in Shakespeare and the other Elizabethans. Other reminiscences might probably be found in Tedaldi-Fores's tragedies by anyone who cared to examine them.

We may mention that, according to Bertana,[1] Edoardo Fabbri, whose early tragedies were purely classical, gave proof of his conversion to the new school in *I Cesenati nel* 1377 (1835–43). The unities are not observed, there

[1] *La Tragedia*, p. 359.

are numerous characters and the People is the hero. Shakespeare's influence is also said to be considerable. Unfortunately, no copy of the play was available in any of the libraries where the writer worked.

But Giovanni Battista Niccolini was distinctly the best of these tragedy-writers after Manzoni and it is worth while tracing his development in detail. Till 1827 he belonged to the strictest sect of the Alfierians. Then he became acquainted with Manzoni and read the chief romantics. In 1828 he delivered a lecture *Dell' Imitazione nell' Arte Drammatica*, in the course of which he remarks that 'if the passions and ideas of Shakespeare's characters are simple and true, we cannot say as much for the way in which they give expression to them in their speeches. He discovers strange and far-fetched relations between things and displays a subtleness in everything he says that spoils the dramatic effect, trying to make comparisons and contrasts out of everything. . . . Nor will my veneration for this very great poet ever induce me to believe that his rhetoric is meant for us Italians.' The difference between French and English tragedy is due, in his opinion, to the fact that the former originated with the men of letters and was by them passed on to the people, whereas the latter originated with the people 'and since the people played a more or less important part in public affairs, it could never forget either its triumphs or its customs, or all that is dear to the national vanity.' He admits, however, that the unity of action is the only one that still matters. For himself, he will neither side with the classics in compressing every story within the limit of twenty-four hours, nor with the romantics in assimilating tragedy to a chronicle. Shakespeare may be able to perform the latter feat, but this is only due to the unifying effect of his great personality.

Indeed, Niccolini's attitude differed very little from that of the other dramatists of the day, with whom he definitely threw in his lot after 1835. He never wavered in his loyalty to the classics, and in a letter of 1841 he called romanticism a plague and the romantic theories illusions. He was well aware that the kind of tragedy which he and his friends wrote was more classic than romantic, being even further removed from Hugo than from Shakespeare, and that this was the only kind possible in Italy. His *Discorso sull' Agamennone d'Eschilo e sulla Tragedia dei Greci e della Nostra* (1844) shows that he was familiar with Shakespeare, whom he calls 'poeta altissimo' and 'sovrano ingegno', praise which reminds one of Manzoni. 'Greek tragedy is romantic,' he says, 'but not like that of the Northern peoples. To this it is superior in the Greeks' exquisite feeling for beauty and in the high philosophic principle that always informed their thought.'

When we turn to the plays themselves, it is difficult to find any trace of Shakespeare's influence. The subject of *Ludovico Sforza* (1834) is not unlike that of *Macbeth* or *Richard III*. The visions that trouble Alfonso (i. 2) are, indeed, of the approved Shakespearean pattern. Ludovico is anxious to remove Galeazzo from his path and seize the throne, and Beatrice d'Este is represented as no less cruel than her husband, but they neither of them owe anything to Shakespeare. Ludovico is the typical monster of cruelty and tyranny of Alfieri's plays. As the story proceeds, the characters become more numerous, it is true, and the scene is frequently changed, but that is all. In *Arnaldo da Brescia* (1843), which is all speeches and no characterization, Niccolini was obviously indebted ultimately to Shakespeare for the size of his canvass. Its lofty patriotism made the play very popular during the Risorgimento, and Gregorovius said it was perhaps the only national play the Italians possess. But Niccolini had been steeped in the classics and Alfieri from his youth up and, as Baldini puts it[1], 'one would say that Niccolini preferred to reproduce Shakespeare by means of the imitations Manzoni has given us of Goethe.' Of direct influence there is no trace.

[1] *Il Teatro di G. B. Niccolini*, p. 590.

X

SHAKESPEARE ON THE ITALIAN STAGE DURING
THE NINETEENTH CENTURY

But though Shakespeare had successfully established his right to rank as a great tragic poet, he was far from having conquered a position upon the Italian stage. 'In Italy, so far as I am aware, no attempt has yet been made to stage performances of this kind' (i. e., romantic plays), says the *Antologia* (August, 1825) in a far from favourable notice of *Hernani*, and this romantic review considers that the reception given to Manzoni's tragedies in Florence augurs ill for the success of the new drama in the theatre.

Adaptations of some of Shakespeare's plays in accordance with the rules were, of course, frequently acted, especially of *Romeo and Juliet* and *Hamlet*. Monti writes indignantly of 'a wretched mangling of Shakespeare's great tragedy' of *Hamlet* in a letter of 1817. And according to Paul Hazard[1] there exists an *Othello ossia lo Slavo* with a happy ending.[2] Nor was Shakespeare neglected by the ballet-writers. Indeed, Capt. W. E. Smyth declared in his *Memoir Descriptive of Sicily and its Islands* that Shakespeare was only known to the public at large by a recent ballet with Macbeth for its subject.[3] This must have been *Macbet, ossia Due Spettri al Convito*, a tragic dance in five acts by Francesco

[1] *La Révolution Française et les Lettres Italiennes*, p. 381.
[2] *Capricci Teatrali*, Vol. III.   [3] *Antologia*, Oct., 1824, p. 107.

Clerico, in which both Duncan's and Banquo's ghosts accuse Macbeth of their murders at the banquet. The subject, we are told, is derived from Shakespeare's play and though the plot of the ballet is differently constructed it is none the less based on the real facts. We have already referred to the vetoing of the ballet of *Hamlet* at Parma ; and Salvatore Viganò, the greatest composer of ballets of the day, brought out tragic dances upon *Othello* and *Coriolanus*. Moreover, *Le Tombe di Verona, ossia Giulietta e Romeo*, a tragic dance in six acts, was produced by Antonio Cherubini at the Canobbiana in Milan in 1830. Needless to say, Shakespeare was still very popular on the operatic stage.

Gustavo Modena is generally considered to have been the greatest and most complete Italian actor of last century. Indeed, Miss Geneviève Ward, who remembers him in *Louis XI*, has recently declared that she considers him the greatest actor she ever saw.[1] He was the father of the modern school of which Tommaso Salvini and Ernesto Rossi, both of whom were his pupils, were the most distinguished members. He produced Schiller's *Maria Stuart* with some success at Venice. But he was less fortunate with *Othello*. Rossi has left a graphic description of the attempt. He was dining with Modena one day in Venice, when he saw *Othello* and *Hamlet* among a heap of plays on a table.

' " Then you have acted these tragedies ? " He looked at me and, with a smile half amused, half bitter, answered, " Yes, yes, I have studied them, but acted them " . . .

[1] Interview in the *Observer*, 18 Nov., 1915.

He took up the manuscript of *Othello*, turned over a few pages and pointed to the first scene. "From here to here." "I don't understand. Was someone taken ill? Was it necessary to abandon the performance?" "Yes, the public was taken ill and we had to let down the curtain." Anxious to give the public something new, he had adapted a translation of *Othello*, suiting it, as far as he could, to the tastes of the day, and taking endless pains with the staging. "But to be frank with you, I had grave doubts as to the result." Rossi was surprised. "Don't you know that the very word Shakespear is hard for us to pronounce? . . . Those blessed rules of Aristotle are firmly fixed in every head. Try to get outside them and you must be prepared for the worst." '

On the night of the performance they were all seized with stage fright, no one more so than Modena. The curtain went up and 'at the scene between Iago and Roderigo, when the latter begins to shout from the street outside Brabantio's house,

What ho, Brabantio! Signior Brabantio, ho!

the audience began to whisper. What is it? A tragedy or a farce?' And when at last Brabantio appeared on the balcony with his clothes all disordered and half asleep, they began to laugh and titter. They had read 'tragedy' on the bill and thought they must be watching a scene from Goldoni or one of Gozzi's *fiabe*. A regular uproar followed and the curtain had to be lowered amid a storm of hisses and whistles.[1] This fiasco gives additional point to a sentence from Dr. Johnson's

[1] Rossi, *Studii Drammatici e Lettere Autobiografiche*, p. 83.

Preface : 'Iago bellows at Brabantio's window, without injury to the scheme of the play, though in terms which a modern audience would not easily endure.' Rossi tells us that the performance took place at the Teatro Re in Milan, at that time the best in Italy. Modena was acting there frequently between 1843 and 1846, but a careful search of the theatrical announcements in the *Gazzetta di Milano* from 1843 to 1848 has not revealed the date. He was, however, always a great admirer of Shakespeare and often quoted Hamlet's advice to the players. He even gave recitations of some passages from *Hamlet*, including 'To be or not to be', using Leoni's translation.

Alemanno Morelli, a good actor, was the next to make the attempt with a performance of *Hamlet* in an adaptation of Rusconi's version at Padua in 1850. It failed to please, but it was not so disastrous as Modena's *Othello*. Success was, however, merely a question of time. 'A great revolution is taking place in literature,' wrote G. B. Niccolini to Salvatore Viale (5 July, 1835). 'The day of Racine's classical tragedy is over, nor does Shakespeare's romantic tragedy seem to suit the age. A great man is wanted to solve the problem and I do not believe myself to be such. The author must educate the public and the public the actors; and where is the public in Italy?'

Ernesto Rossi was destined to be 'the first to interpret Shakespeare successfully upon the Italian stage,' as Cavour expressed it in a letter of introduction.[1]

---

[1] Rossi, *Quarant' Anni di Vita Artistica*, Vol. I. p. 154.

[*To face p.* 155.

ERNESTO ROSSI AS 'HAMLET'.

He spent the whole night over the two plays he had found on Modena's table. But in these hotch-potch versions from Leoni 'there was nothing but the name of Shakespeare. I venture to say that they proved clearly that the interpreter was not convinced of his poet and that the great artist had been too much concerned with the times, the taste, habits and customs of the public.' In any case, Leoni did not satisfy him. Rusconi's prose *Hamlet* was quite to his taste, but he thought that *Othello* should be in verse and therefore approached Carcano, several of whose versions of single plays he had read. The requisite translation was ready in 1852. Then, in 1855, he was in Paris with Ristori, when the Wallack company from South America gave some performances of Shakespeare. He had began to learn English and found he could follow with the help of Rusconi. He also paid a flying visit to London to see Charles Kean, Edmund's son, in *Richard III*. He was well received by the English actor, who gave him acting versions of *Hamlet* and *Othello* and other plays, which were afterwards of the greatest assistance to him. Then, in the spring of 1856, he fulfilled his great ambition and avenged his master, Modena, by playing *Othello* at the Teatro Re in Milan. The performance was a real success and was repeated several times.

A fortnight later he produced *Hamlet* equally success-fully. He gives the following interesting details in his essay on the play.[1] 'While I was studying *Hamlet* I could not understand or clearly explain the Prince's

[1] *Studii Drammatici*, p. 328.

appearance in the churchyard before I played the part. It seemed to me something forced, far-fetched, unnatural; and I went to the theatre to dress, I can still remember, quite preoccupied with the idea. In spite of the great success of the four preceding acts, I was still struggling with my doubts and uncertainties in my dressing-room. I hardly listened to those good friends of mine who had come behind the scenes and were congratulating me on the success of the strange tragedy, as they called it. On the curtain going up for the fifth act, which represented the churchyard, I took the few steps from my dressing-room to the wings, weary in body and mind. But when I heard the grave-digger sing those verses and roll out the skulls and carelessly throw out the bones which, though only made of cardboard, looked to me like human bones and skulls, a shudder ran through my whole body and I felt a chilly tear in my eye. My foot guided my body forward, not my mind my foot. Thank God, I thought to myself. Now I understand; the riddle is solved; my doubts have vanished; this is nature, not artifice. Hamlet is tired, as I am. The churchyard is his home, the well-deserved resting-place, peace, silence, oblivion. First Ophelia, then Hamlet; separated in life, united in death. I played the fifth act as I then knew how, and could, with conviction, my mind altogether absorbed by the author and character. From that evening the churchyard scene was always one of my greatest artistic triumphs.'

Thus was the churchyard scene, made famous by Voltaire, understood at the eleventh hour by the first successful Italian Hamlet. This anecdote explains why Rossi was so well fitted to introduce Shakespeare to the Italian stage. His acting was not in accordance with our ideas and his visits to London in 1876 and to the United States were not successes. But he was long regarded as the best Hamlet in Italy and is still often so considered. Garibaldi saw him in the part in 1866 at Genoa and sent for him to his box. 'This *Hamlet*', he told him, 'has moved me profoundly. Every nerve in my body is quivering. He is no myth, he is a man! I read the play a long time ago. I liked it, but it did not interest me and it did not impress me as it has this evening.' Then he told Rossi to leave him. 'I don't want to see you or speak to you again, I want to remain in my illusion.' 'The performance lasted till midnight, but the General remained at his post like a dead sentinel. The next morning, when I went to see him, he said: "That Shakespeare is a great magician. He kept me awake all night. If he does the same to you, you cannot sleep much."'[1] 'I saw him in *Hamlet* when he was an old man at Florence,' writes Luigi Rasi, the greatest authority on the history of the Italian stage, of Rossi.[2] 'A colossus! Shakespear appeared to me in all his greatness. Rossi was a mighty, measureless poem, such as I had never seen, nor ever saw again.'

In 1858 Rossi played Macbeth at Venice and Lear at Turin. Lear was one of his best parts, and won him admiration even in London. Coriolanus, Shylock and Romeo were among his other Shakespearean parts. *Julius*

[1] *Quarant' Anni*, &c., Vol. I. p. 233. [2] *I Comici Italiani*, II. 430.

Cæsar he never played, to his great regret in his old age, probably owing to his dislike of Roman plays ; for he was a romantic to the core. But these performances were, as a rule, appreciated by the few rather than by the general public, which was still loyal to the old classical plays. *Hamlet* and *Othello* were always the most popular. Rossi was, however, the first, according to Angelo de Gubernatis,[1] to make a firm stand against this indifference, 'to persevere steadily till the English theatre was firmly established on our stage, to overcome the many obstacles which stood in the way of its representation.' Rossi has left ample proof of his genuine love of Shakespeare in the prose translation of *Julius Cæsar* in the *Studii Drammatici*, as well as in the studies of Shakespearean characters in that work and the *Quarant' Anni di Vita Artistica*. He even called his villa at Leghorn Villa Shakespeare.

Tommaso Salvini was, of course, a greater actor than Rossi, but he was less intellectual. In his early days he preferred Voltaire to Shakespeare. Then once again, in 1853, Shakespeare's works fell into his hands, but he admits that, even on second reading, his characters, his ideas and his form struck him as so strange that he hesitated whether he should study him or not.[2] But he persevered and, encouraged probably by Rossi's success, he appeared as Othello at Vicenza in June, 1856, and then in Venice, where he received an ovation. Hamlet and King Lear were his next parts. But even *Othello* was not at that time really popular, though it is generally

---

[1] Introduction to Rossi's *Studii Drammatici*.   [2] *Autobiography*, p. 77.

regarded as Salvini's greatest part, much less the other two. Ristori first played Lady Macbeth in Carcano's translation in London in 1857. Thus by 1860, when Italy ceased to be a geographical expression and first really became a nation, Shakespeare had obtained a place in the repertoire of the three greatest actors of the day, whose work was appreciated outside Italy; for Rossi was much admired in South America as well as in most continental countries.

Another factor which must have done something to create an atmosphere favourable to Shakespeare in Italy at this time was L. Gualtieri's five act play, *Shakespeare*, published at Milan in 1858. Rossi included it in his repertoire. We are behind the scenes at the ' Blakfriars ' Theatre during the first performance of *Romeo and Juliet*, which poverty has obliged Shakespeare to sell to the foolish Lord Makensie. Burbage is too drunk to act, and Shakespeare, who is in love with the Juliet, comes forward and plays the part with brilliant success, thereby clearly proving his authorship. Elizabeth witnesses the performance and takes a fancy to him, since he is so like Essex. He makes love to her, believing that she is Lady Makensie, but offends her by reciting a poem referring to Mary Queen of Scots and Anne Boleyne. Shakespeare is committed to the Tower and condemned to death. Thoughout the play he talks in a bombastic, epigrammatic style which is probably meant to resemble that of *Hamlet*, the play upon which he is apparently engaged in prison. He repeats ' Essere o non essere, ecco il gran problema ', Rusconi's version of ' To be or not to be '.

Then he endeavours to pull himself together with 'Coraggio, William . . . William, William, remember Socrates.' His fellow-actors appear to bid him farewell. He informs them that he has learnt Dante by heart and he has apparently been reading Mazzini, for he declares that Dante, 'a divine poet, has composed the poem of faith, I, poor mortal, that of doubt.' And he proceeds to give them Hamlet's advice to the players. Then the Queen enters, saying that she has merely provided him with a comedy or drama, not, of course, as good as his own. But perhaps it is as well that, instead of everyone being killed, as in one of his tragedies, there is not to be a single death. The play is interesting, for all its absurdities. Lord Southampton and Ben Jonson are among the characters. It must have done not a little to familiarize the Italian theatre-going public with Shakespeare and his times.

Though Shakespeare has, of course, never had a tithe of the influence in a Latin country like Italy that he has exercised in Germany, he is more frequently played there than in France. For one thing, with the single exception of Alfieri, Italy has produced no great national dramatic poet to set against him, and in a land where a gift for acting is so universal, Shakespeare's tragedies offer far too splendid a field to the actor for there to be the least danger of his being neglected, once this had been recognized. He was slow in making his way at first, but the influence of time, the springing up of a generation that knew not the unities and the perseverance of his interpreters, especially of Rossi, gradually wore down the old prejudices till he was firmly established on the Italian stage. To appear as Hamlet and Othello is the ambition of every would-be tragic actor in the peninsula. Both these parts have been played by Ermete Zacconi, for instance, who even got as far as rehearsing *Much Ado About Nothing* when he had the great actress Emma Gramatica in his company. He also had thoughts of producing *Measure for Measure*. He it was who introduced *The Taming of the Shrew* to his countrymen. But the part of Petruchio will now always be connected with the name of Ermete Novelli, the greatest of living Italian actors. Like Salvini's son, Gustavo, who also plays Hamlet and Othello, Novelli has appeared as Shylock in a poor adaptation of the *Merchant of Venice*, which has long been popular on the Italian stage. *Romeo and Juliet* is not infrequently acted, while the Compagnia Stabile di Roma has brought out *Julius Cæsar* and *King Lear* at the Teatro Argentina.

But undoubtedly the most remarkable Shakespearean revival in Italy of recent years was that of the *Midsummer Night's Dream* in Diego Angeli's version at the Teatro Argentina in Rome by the same company during the carnival of 1910. It was elaborately staged and played in its entirety with Mendelssohn's music to crowded houses for twenty-two consecutive evenings—a very long run for Rome. In the following year it was given successfully at Milan. German films of the *Tempest* and *Winter's Tale* have made their appearance at the Kinema theatres.

Ristori was a great Lady Macbeth, but Shakespeare

M

does not appeal to the modern Italian actress brought up on Dumas Fils and Sardou. 'Oui, Shakespeare . . . c'est toujours le Dieu,' said Eleonora Duse to Count Primoli. 'Mais—à part quelques créations sublimes qui ne sont guère dans mes cordes—généralement chez lui les rôles de femme sont sacrifiés. . . . Si, de son temps, il avait eu une artiste comme Sarah, quel rôle il aurait créé pour elle!'

However, in the popular theatres, where the prices of admission range from 30 to 50 centesimi, and Æschylus, Sophocles and Euripides draw large audiences, Shakespeare is one of the chief attractions. So at least Miss Helen Zimmern tells us.[1] Hence in the streets of the large towns you are quite likely to hear a work-man in shirt sleeves or a coster pushing a barrow repeating to himself, 'To be or not to be', or speeches of Othello or Lady Macbeth, in his native dialect, with additions or changes introduced to suit the speaker's memory or taste. 'It is most amusing at these repre-sentations to note the costumes worn by the actors. Once I saw Hamlet dressed in a velvet shooting-suit, modified for the occasion, which he had borrowed from one of the audience, who in return was admitted free of charge.'

The acting in these theatres and, indeed, in most of the Italian performances, would be sniffed at in England as belonging to the old-fashioned declamatory school, over the disappearance of which we are in the habit of pluming ourselves. Yet, in spite of its defects, this

[1] *Italy of the Italians*, p. 173.

declamatory style was all to the advantage of a poet as rhetorical as Shakespeare. So long as it prevailed, his great tragedies were acted regularly in every kind of theatre in England and were therefore far better known to the lower classes than they can be to-day. Whatever its advantages, the change in taste has resulted in the disappearance of Shakespearean tragedy from the popular repertoires; and a play like *Richard III*, which was enjoyed by and known to every coachman or footman in the days of our fathers, is now hardly ever acted. Can we still say, as Jane Austen did in *Mansfield Park*, that Shakespeare is part of an Englishman's constitution?

The present writer has never seen these Shakespeare performances at the popular theatres in Italy, but he saw *Hamlet* at the little Southern mountain town of La Cava dei Tirreni in 1904. Hamlet belonged altogether to the old school and would not have been tolerated for a moment in England. Some of his business was highly characteristic. When he remarked to Ophelia, 'God hath given you one face and you make yourselves another', he rubbed the corner of his long black cloak on Ophelia's rouged and powdered cheek and held it up to the applauding audience. The acting was good throughout, for the level is always high in Italy, even in such small provincial companies. But Ophelia stood out above the rest. The enthusiastic audience was obviously thoroughly familiar with the play. 'Essere o non essere'—for the version was, as usual, Rusconi's —was loudly cheered and Hamlet was hissed when he refused to kill the King at his prayers.

But a love of Shakespeare such as prevailed during the Romantic movement must always be the exception in Italy. Even an Englishman who ranks Dante above all other poets is rarely a whole-hearted enthusiast for Shakespeare, however fully he may realize his greatness. And in Italy Dante is, of course, the poet of poets. Humour is a plant too redolent of the soil upon which it grows to be safely exported. The comedies are rarely read and still more rarely acted. Even Falstaff the unabashed can never feel quite at his ease in an Italian doublet and hose, however excellent the cut. The average Italian thinks of Shakespeare primarily as a tragic poet and there will always be something strange and incomprehensible, something exotic to a Latin about *King Lear*, for instance, or *Hamlet*. Yet when Shakespeare is speaking the universal language of the passions, as in *Othello* or *Romeo and Juliet*, he goes straight to the heart of an Italian audience. Not only do these plays appeal to the national feeling, since they have Verona and Venice for their setting, but the genuinely Italian character of the jealousy and love they depict is at once recognized and appreciated ; Italy and England were never more closely akin than during the 'spacious days,' and it would be strange indeed if Shakespeare lost his hold upon the hearts of a people which he has painted to the life, now that

> A Roman and a British ensign wave
> Friendly together.

APPENDIX

Contents of *Saggi di Eloquenza Estratti dal Teatro di Shakespeare* (Milan, 1811)

Tempest, ii. 1. 'Sir, he may live . . . as stooping to relieve him.'

Coriolanus, i. 3. 'I pray you, daughter, sing . . . have found issue.'

Coriolanus, ii. 1. 'All tongues speak of him . . . posture.'

Hamlet, iii. 1. 'To be, or not to be . . . '

Hamlet, iv. 7. 'There is a willow . . . muddy death.'

Antony and Cleopatra, ii. 2. 'The barge she sat in . . . wharfs.'

2 Henry IV, iii. 1. 'How many thousands . . . deny it to a king.'

Henry V, iv. Chorus, to 'morning name.'

2 Henry VI, iii. 2. 'See how the blood . . . probable.'

2 Henry VI, iii. 3. 'How fares my lord . . . meditation.'

Richard III, i. 1. 'Now is the winter . . . lute.'

Richard III, iv. 3. 'The tyrannous . . . framed.'

Henry VIII, ii. 2. 'Commend me to his grace . . . monument.'

Winter's Tale, i. 2. 'We were as twinn'd . . . ours.'

Twelfth Night, ii. 4. 'She never told . . . monument.'

Merchant of Venice, v. 1. 'How sweet the moonlight . . . hear it.'

Merchant of Venice, iv. 1. 'The quality of mercy . . . deeds of mercy.'

Twelfth Night, i. 1. 'If music . . . high fantastical.'

Winter's Tale, iv. 3. 'Now, my fairest friend . . . o'er and o'er.'

Titus Andronicus, ii. 3. 'My lovely Aaron . . . babe asleep.'

Midsummer Night's Dream, i. 1. 'Therefore, fair Hermia . . . single blessedness.'

Midsummer Night's Dream, v. 2. Buck [*sic*] 'Now the hungry lion . . . to frolic.'

BIBLIOGRAPHY

Only books which have actually yielded results are included. The author has not himself examined those marked *.

WORKS OF SPECIAL IMPORTANCE FOR THE SUBJECT

BELLEZZA, PAOLO—'Gli Studi Shakespeariani del Manzoni,' *Giornale Storico della Letteratura Italiana*, Torino, 1898.

BERTANA, EMILIO—'Il Teatro Tragico Italiano del Secolo XVIII prima dell' Alfieri,' *Giornale Storico della Letteratura Italiana*, Supplemento IV, Torino, 1901. See especially the note on page 73.

GRAF, ARTURO—*L'Anglomania e l'Influsso Inglese in Italia nel Secolo XVIII*, chap. xiii, Torino, 1911. [The best and fullest authority for the eighteenth century.]

MAZZONI, GUIDO—*L'Ottocento*, Milano, 1913.

MORANDI, LUIGI—*Voltaire contro Shakespeare e Baretti contro Voltaire*, Città di Castello, 1884.

MUONI, GUIDO—*I Drammi dello Shakespeare e la Critica Romantica Italiana (1815–45)*, Firenze, 1908.

SCHERILLO, MICHELE—'Ammiratori e Imitatori dello Shakespeare prima del Manzoni,' *Nuova Antologia*, Firenze, April, 1885.

SCHIAVELLO, GIUSEPPE—*La Fama dello Shakespeare nel Secolo XVIII*, Camerino, 1904.

OTHER WORKS

ALFIERI, VITTORIO—*Opere*, 22 Vols., Italia (Pisa), 1805–15. *Opere Scelte, cioè la vita, scritta da esso, tutte le tragedie, colle lettere di Calsabigi, di Cesarotti e le risposte dell' Autore*, Paris, 1847.

ALGAROTTI, FRANCESCO—*Opere*, 17 Vols., Venezia, 1792. [Letters in Vols. IX–X.]

ANDRES, GIOVANNI—*Dell' Origine, Progressi e Stato Attuale di Ogni Letteratura*, Parma, 1782–1822.

ARTEAGA, STEFANO—*Le Rivoluzioni del Teatro Musicale Italiano dalla sua Origine fino al Presento*, Venezia, 1785.

BALDINI, MASSIMO—*Il Teatro di G. B. Niccolini*, Firenze, 1907.

BARETTI, MARCANTONIO GIUSEPPE—*Opere*, Milano, 1822. *Discours sur Shakespeare et sur Monsieur de Voltaire* (ed. F. Biondelillo), Lanciano, 1911. *Prefazioni e Polemiche* (ed. L. Piccioni), Bari, 1911. [Contains the 'Discours sur Shakespeare'.]

BATTAGLIA, GIACINTO—*Mosaïco, Saggi diversi di Critica Drammatica*, Milano, 1845.

BEDUSCHI, ANTONIO—*Sullo Stato Attuale della Tragedia in Italia*, Parma, 1827.

BENEDETTI, FRANCESCO—*Opere*, 2 Vols., Firenze, 1858.

BERCHET, GIOVANNI—*Lettera Simiseria di Grisostomo*, Milano, 1816.

BERTANA, EMILIO—*La Tragedia*, Milano, 1904-5. *V. Alfieri Studiato nella Vita, nel Pensiere e nell' Arte*, Torino, 1904.

BERTÒLA, AURELIO—*Idea della Bella Letteratura Alemanna*, Lucca, 1784.

BETTINELLI, SAVERIO—*Opere Edite e Inedite in Poesia ed in Versi*, 24 Vols., Venezia, 1799-1801.

*BICCHERAI—*Tragedia e Considerazioni sul Teatro Italiano*, Firenze, 1767.

BLAIR, HUGH—*Lezioni di Rettorica e Belle Lettere*, Tradotte e commentate da F. Soave, 3 Vols., Parma, 1801-2.

BONAFEDE, APPIANO—*Il Bue Pedagogo, Novelle Menippee di Luciano di Firenzuola contra una certa Frusta Pseudoepigrafa di Aristarco Scannabue*, Milano, 1830.

BONAZZI, LUIGI—*Gustavo Modena e l'arte sua*, Città di Castello, 1884.

BORSA, MATTEO—'Saggio Filosofico sopra la Musica Imitativa Teatrale,' in *Opuscoli Scelti sulla Scienza*, Vol. IV (1781), Milano, 1778, &c.

CANTÙ, CESARE—*Corrispondenze di Diplomatici della Repubblica e del Regno d'Italia (1796–1814)*, Milano, 1884.

CARCANO, GIULIO—*Opere Complete*, with Memoir, 10 Vols., Milan, 1892.

CARRER, LUIGI—*Anello di Sette Gemme a Venezia*, Venezia, 1838. Article on Giustina Renier-Michiel in *Biografia degli Italiani illustri nelle scienze, lettere ed arti nel secolo XVIII e dei contemporanei*, Venezia, 1835.

CERRETTI, LUIGI—*Istituzioni di Eloquenza*, Milano, 1811.

CESAROTTI, MELCHIORRE—*Opere*, 40 Vols., Firenze, 1808. *Cento Lettere Inedite a Giustina Renier-Michiel*, Ancona, 1884.

CHATFIELD-TAYLOR, H. C.—*Goldoni, a Biography*, London, 1914.

COLAGROSSO, FRANCESCO—*La Prima Tragedia di Antonio Conti*, Firenze, 1898.

CONCARI, TULLIO—*Il Settecento*, Milano, 1900.

CONTI, ANTONIO—*Giulio Cesare*, Faenza, 1726. *Il Riccio Rapito del Sig. Alessandro Pope, tradotto dall' Inglese*, London, 1751.

CORNIANI, GIAMBATTISTA—*I Secoli della Letteratura Italiana dopo il suo Risorgimento*, 9 Vols., Brescia, 1804–13.

CRISTOFORIS, G. B. DE—*Sergianni Caracciolo*, Milano, 1826.

DANDOLO, GIROLAMO—*La Caduta della Repubblica di Venezia*, Venezia, 1855.

DEJOB, CHARLES—*Madame de Stael et l'Italie*, Paris, 1896.

DENINA, CARLO—*Discorso sopra le Vicende della Letteratura*, Torino, 1760.

DUCIS, JEAN FRANÇOIS—*Œuvres*, 3 Vols., Paris, 1826.

FEDERICI, CAMILIO—'Il Duca di Borgogna, o siano I Falsi Galantuomini,' *Opere*, Vol. VII, Firenze, 1827.

FERMI, STEFANO—*Lorenzo Magalotti, Scienziato e Letterato (1637–1712)*, Piacenza, 1903.

FOSCOLO, UGO—*Opere Edite e Postume*, 12 Vols., Firenze, 1850–90. *Lettere Inedite del Foscolo, del Giordani e della Signora di Stael a Vincenzo Monti*, Livorno, 1876.

GALLETTI, ALFREDO—'Manzoni, Shakespeare e Bossuet,' *Studi di Filologia Moderna*, Pisa, July–December, 1911.

GHERARDINI, GIOVANNI—*Elementi di Poesia ad Uso delle Scuole*, Milano, 1820.

GIORDANI, PIETRO—*Opere*, Vol. IV, Milano, 1854.

GOLDONI, CARLO—*Collezione Completa delle Commedie*, 30 Vols., Prato, 1819–21. *Mémoires de M. Goldoni pour servir à l'histoire de sa Vie, et à celle de son Théâtre*, 3 Vols., Paris, 1787.

GOZZI, CARLO—*Opere Edite e Inedite*, 14 Vols., Venezia, 1803.

*GRIMALDI, RAIMONDO—*Saggio sulla Tragedia*, Napoli, 1813.

GRITTI, FRANCESCO—'Amleto, Tragedia del Signor Ducis,' *Teatro Moderno Applaudito*, Vol. II.

GUALTIERI, LUIGI—*Shakespeare, dramma in cinque atti, con Prologo*, Milano, 1858.

HAZARD, PAUL—*La Révolution Française et les Lettres Italiennes*, Paris, 1910. 'Les Littératures du Nord et l'Esprit Latin en Italie,' in *Studien zur Vergleichenden Litteraturgeschichte*, Vol. IX (ed. Dr. Max Koch), Berlin, 1901, &c.

JOHNSON, SAMUEL—Preface to his *Shakespeare*, London, 1765.

JUSSERAND, JULES A. A. J.—*Shakespeare en France sous l'Ancien Régime*, Paris, 1898.

KELLY, MICHAEL—*Reminiscences*, 2 Vols., London, 1826.

KERBAKER, M.—*Shakespeare et Goethe nei versi di V. Monti*, Firenze, 1897.

KING, BOLTON—*The Life of Mazzini*, London, 1911.

LAMBERTI, LUIGI—*L'Edipo Re, Tragedia di Sofocle, in versi italiani*, Parma, 1796.

LANDAU, MARCUS—*Geschichte der Italienischen Litteratur im achtzehnten Jahrhundert*, Berlin, 1899.

LEOPARDI, GIACOMO—*Pensieri di Varia Filosofia e di Bella Letteratura*, 7 Vols., Firenze, 1898.

LETI, GREGORIO—*Del Teatro Britanico, o vero Historia dello Stato Antico e Presente, Corte, Governo . . . Leggi . . . Religione & Avvenimenti della Grande Brettagna*, 2 Vols., London, 1683.

LE TOURNEUR, P. F.—*Shakespeare Traduit de l'Anglais*, 20 Vols., Paris, 1776–82.

LOUNSBURY, THOMAS R.—*Shakespeare and Voltaire* (Yale Bicentennial Publications), 1911.

LUCHAIRE, JULIEN—*Essai sur l'Evolution Intellectuelle de l'Italie de 1815 à 1830*, Paris, 1906.

LUGNANI, GIUSEPPE—'Macbet' in Vol. II of his *Tragedie*, Venezia, 1817.

*MAFFEI, SCIPIONE—*Osservazioni Letterarie*, Verona, 1737.

MALAMANNI, VITTORIO—'Giustina Renier-Michiel, i suoi Amici, il suo Tempo,' in *Archivio Veneto*, Vol. 38.

MANZONI, ALESSANDRO—*Opere Complete*, Paris, 1843. *Opere Varie*, Milano, 1845. *Opere Inedite o Rare*, 6 Vols., Milano, 1883–98. *Carteggio*, Milano, 1912. *The Betrothed Lovers* (Translated by Rev. C. Swan), 3 Vols., Pisa, 1828.

MARENCO, CARLO—*Bondelmonte e gli Amedei*, Torino, 1827. *Corso Donati*, Torino, 1830. *Ezzelino Terzo*, Torino, 1832. *Due Nuove Tragedie*, Torino, 1835. *Pia de' Tolomei*, Torino, 1837. *Berengario Augusto*, Torino, 1840. *Tragedie Inedite*, Firenze, 1856. *Tragedie*, 2 Vols., Torino, 1859.

MARENCO, VINCENZO—*Lo Spirito di Patriottismo riguardo alle Scienze e alla Letteratura*, Torino, 1783.

MARTINELLI, VINCENZO—*Istoria Critica della Vita Civile*, London, 1752.

MASI, ERNESTO—*Studi sulla storia del Teatro Italiano nel Secolo XVIII*, Firenze, 1891.

MAZZINI, GIUSEPPE—*Opere Edite e Inedite*, Vol. III, Milano, Roma, Firenze, 1861–1904.

MAZZUCHETTI, LAVINIA—*Schiller in Italia*, Milano, 1913.

MENEGHELLI, PIETRANTONIO—*Dissertazione sopra la Tragedia Cittadinesca*, Padova, 1795.

METASTASIO, PIETRO—*Opere*, Vol. XII, Paris, 1782. *Opere Postume*, 3 Vols., Venezia, 1795.

MILIZIA, FRANCESCO—*Trattato Completo, Formale e Materiale del Teatro*, Venezia, 1794.

MONTAGU, ELIZABETH—*Saggio sugli Scritti e sul Genio di Shakespeare*, Firenze, 1828.

MONTI, VINCENZO—*Opere Inedite e Rare*, 5 Vols., Milano, 1832. *Prose e Poesie*, 5 Vols., Firenze, 1847.

NAPOLI-SIGNORELLI, PIETRO—*Storia Critica de' Teatri Antichi e Moderni*, Napoli, 1777. *Elementi di Poesia Drammatica*, Milano, Anno X (1801).

NICCOLINI, GIOVANNI BATTISTA—*Arnaldo da Brescia*, 1843. *Opere*, 3 Vols., Firenze, 1858.

* *Osservazioni fatte da un Viaggiatore in Alcuni Paesi d'Europa*, Lucca, 1787.

PAGANI-CESA, G. U.—*Sopra il Teatro Tragico Italiano*, Firenze, 1825.

PELLICO, SILVIO—*Epistolario*, Firenze, 1856. *Opere Complete*, Milano, 1857.

PEPOLI, ALESSANDRO—*Tragedie*, 6 Vols., Venezia, 1787.

PIGNOTTI, LORENZO—*La Tomba di Shakespeare*, Firenze, 1779.

PINDEMONTE, GIOVANNI—*Componimenti Teatrali*, 4 Vols., Venezia, 1804–5.

PINDEMONTE, IPPOLITO—*Arminio, edizione settima. S'aggiungono Tre Discorsi*, Verona, 1819. 'Elogio di LeonardoTarga,' in *Eloggi di Letterati*, Vol. I, Verona, 1825.

PIOZZI, HESTER LYNCH—*Observations and Reflections made in the course of a Journey through France, Italy and Germany*, London, 1789.

* *Poesie Scelte*, Firenze, 1804.

PONTE, LORENZO DA—*Memorie*, 3 Vols., Nuova-Jorca, 1829-30.

PORENA, MANFREDI—*V. Alfieri e la Tragedia*, Milano, 1904.

PRIMOLI, GIUSEPPE—'La Duse,' in *Revue de Paris*, June, 1897.

QUADRIO, FRANCESCO SAVERIO—*Della Storia e della Ragione d'Ogni Poesia*, Milano, 1743–52.

RAMIREZ, GIUSEPPE—'Le Tombe di Verona, dramma del Cittadino Mercier, Traduzione,' in *Teatro Moderno Applaudito*, Vol. XII.

RASI, LUIGI—*I Comici Italiani. Biografia, Bibliografia, Iconografia*, 2 Vols., Firenze, 1897, 1905.

REINA, FRANCESCO—*Vita di Giuseppe Parini*, Milano, 1811.

RICCARDI, ANTONIO—*Manuale di Ogni Letteratura*, Milano, 1831.

RICCOBONI, LOUIS—*Réflexions historiques et critiques sur les différens théâtres de l'Europe*, Paris, 1738.

RINIERI, ILARIO—*Della Vita e delle Opere di Silvio Pellico*, 3 Vols., Torino, 1898.

RISTORI, ADELAIDE—*Studies and Memories*, London, 1888.

ROBERTI, GIAMBATTISTA—*Opere*, Vols. VIII and IX, Bassano, 1797.

ROBERTSON, J. G.—'Shakespeare on the Continent' in *Cambridge History of English Literature* (Cambridge, 1910), Vol. V. pp. 283 and 456.

ROLLI, PAOLO—*Remarks upon M. Voltaire's Essay on the Epick Poetry of the European Nations*, London, 1728. *Del Paradiso Perduto, Traduzione*, London, 1735.

ROSSI, ERNESTO—*Studii Drammatici e Lettere Autobiografiche*, Firenze, 1885. *Quarant'Anni di Vita Artistica*, 3 Vols., Firenze, 1887.

SALVINI, TOMMASO—*Leaves from the Autobiography of*, London, 1893.

SANCTIS, FRANCESCO DE—*Storia della Letteratura Italiana* (ed. B. Croce), 2 Vols., Bari, 1912.

SCHLEGEL, A. W. VON—*A Course of Lectures on Dramatic Art and Literature*, London, 1846.

SHEFFIELD, JOHN (DUKE OF BUCKINGHAMSHIRE)—*Works*, London, 1753.

SHERLOCK, MARTIN—*Letters from an English Traveller*, 2 Vols., London, 1802.

SMITH, D. NICHOL—*Eighteenth Century Essays on Shakespeare*, Glasgow, 1903.

SPINELLI, GIAMBATTISTA CARRARA—*Versi e Prose*, Milano, 1827.

STAEL, MADAME DE—*Corinne*. 'Sulla Memoria e l'Utilità delle Traduzioni,' in *Biblioteca Italiana*, Jan. and June, 1816.

Teatro Moderno Applaudito and its continuation, *L'Anno Teatrale*, 111 Vols., Venezia, 1796–1809.

TEDALDI-FORES, CARLO—*I Fieschi e I Doria*, Milano, 1829. *Epistola a Cesare Arici*, 1822.

TEXTE, JOSEPHE—*Jean-Jacques Rousseau et les Origines du Cosmopolitisme Littéraire*, Paris, 1895.

TORTI, GIOVANNI—*Poesie Complete*, Genova, 1853.

VALLE, CESARE DELLA (DUCA DI VENTIGNANO)—*Giulietta e Romeo*, Roma, 1826.

VERONESE, ANGELA (AGLAJA ANASSILLIDE)—*Versi, aggiuntevi le notizie della sua vita scritte da lei medesima*, Padova, 1826.

VERRI, ALESSANDRO—*Carteggio di Pietro e di Alessandro Verri*, Milano, 1910. *Lettere e Scritte Inedite di Pietro e di Alessandro Verri*, 2 Vols., Milano, 1879–80. *Vicende Memorabili dal 1789 al 1801* (with Maggi's 'Life' prefixed), Reggio, Modena, 1858.

VOLTAIRE, F. M. AROUET DE—*Essai sur la Poésie Epique*, 1728. *Lettres Philosophiques*, 1734; and Letters in *Œuvres Complètes*, 54 Vols., Paris, 1883–5.

WALKER, JOSEPH COOPER—*Historical Memoir of Italian Tragedy*, London, 1799.

ZENO, APOSTOLO—'Ambleto,' in *Poesie Drammatiche*, Vol. IX, Venezia, 1744.

ZIMMERN, HELEN—*Italy of the Italians*, London, 1914.

ZUMBINI, B.—*Sulle Poesie di Vincenzo Monti*, Firenze, 1894.

PERIODICALS

L'Accattabrighe, ossia Classico-Romantico-Machia, Milano, Nov. 1818–March 1819.

* *Annali Letterari d'Italia*, Vol. I. Pt. 1, 175–.

Antologia, Firenze, 1821–30.

Biblioteca Italiana, Milano, 1816–31.

Il Conciliatore, Milano, 1818–9.

Il Corriere delle Dame, Milano, 1810–17.

Giornale Enciclopedico di Firenze, Firenze and Roma, 1809–14.

Jahrbuch der deutschen Shakespeare-Gesellschaft, Vol. XXXVII (Shakespeare's Werke in der Musik), Berlin, Weimar.

Nuova Antologia, Firenze, 1866, &c.

* *Nuovo Giornale dei Letterati d'Italia*, Vol. XXXII, 1785.

Nuovo Giornale Letterario d'Italia, Vol. XX, Modena, 1789.

Nuovo Ricoglitore, Milano, 1825–30.

Il Poligrafo, Milano, 1811–4.

Il Raccoglitore, Milano, 1819–22

Le Spectateur, ou le Socrate Moderne, où l'on voit un portrait naïf des mœurs de ce Siècle. Traduit de l'Anglais, 5 Vols., Amsterdam, 1746.

Lo Spettatore, ossia varietà istoriche, letterarie, critiche, politiche, morali, del Signor Malte-Brun recate in Italiano, Milano, 1815.

La Vespa. Giornale di Scienze, Lettere ed Arti, che succede all' Ape Italiana, Milano, 1807–8.

ITALIAN TRANSLATIONS OF SHAKESPEARE CONSULTED

ANGELI, DIEGO—*Teatro di Guglielmo Shakespeare. Nuova Traduzione,* Milano, 1911, &c. [In progress.]

CARCANO, GIULIO—*Opere di Shakespeare,* 12 Vols., Milano, 1875–81. And other editions and separate versions of single plays.

LEONI, MICHELE—*Giulio Cesare, Tragedia di Guglielmo Shakespeare, tradotta dall' originale inglese in versi italiani,* Milano, 1811. *Tragedie di Shakespeare,* 14 Vols., Verona, 1819. Also separate versions of single plays.

NICCOLINI, GIUSEPPE—*Macbet, Tragedia di Guglielmo Shakespeare,* Brescia, 1830.

RENIER-MICHIEL, GIUSTINA—*Opere drammatiche di Shakespeare volgarizzate da una cittadina veneta.* Tom I (*Othello*), Venezia, 1797 or 1798? Tom II (*Macbeth*), Venezia, 1798. Tom III (*Coriolanus*), Venezia, 1800.

RUSCONI, CARLO—*Teatro Completo di Shakespeare tradotto dall' originale inglese in Prosa Italiana,* 2 Vols. with continuous pagination, Padova, 1838.

Shakespeare, Saggi di Eloquenza estratti dal Teatro di, Milano, 1811.

VALENTINI, DOMENICO—*Il Giulio Cesare, Tragedia Istorica di Guglielmo Shakespeare, tradotta dall' Inglese in Lingua Toscana,* Siena, 1756.

VALLETTA, IGNAZIO—*Giulio Cesare, Tragedia di Shakespeare, recata in Italiano,* Firenze, 1829. *Otello,* Firenze, 1830. *Coriolano,* Firenze, 1834.

INDEX

INDEX

Addison, Joseph 8, 16, 24, 27-8, 29, 33, 40, 49, 50, 51, 52, 84, 94, 96, 101, 128, 130

Alfieri, V. 14, 44, 45, 62–5, 67, 74, 83, 84, 96, 105, 108, 122, 125, 127

Algarotti, F. . 18–9, 32, 73

Anassillide, Aglaja *see* Veronese, A.

Andres, Giov. . . 27–9, 102

Angeli, Diego . 137–8, 161

Arteaga, S. 24

Barbieri, G. 134

Baretti, G. 14, 31–2, 33, 34, 38, 46–55, 57

Battaglia, G. . . . 134, 136

Bazzoni, G. 134

Beduschi, Ant. . . 127, 142

Benedetti, F. . . . 107, 111

Berchet, G. 103, 121

Bertola, A. 26–7

Bertolotti, D. . . . 95, 129

Bettinelli, S. . . . 21–2, 86

Biccherai, ... 43

Biffi, G. 43

Blair, Hugh 42, 91

Bonafede, A. 47–8

Borsa, M. 45, 46

Botta, C. 131

Brême, L. de . . . 99, 131

Calsabigi, R. dei 44–5, 63, 64

Caminer-Turra, E. . . 66–7

Carcano, G. 136–7, 155, 159

Caruso, L. 82

Cerretti, L. . . . 83, 86, 92

Cesarotti, M. 22–3, 27, 34, 40, 76, 78

Cherubini, A. 152

Conti, A. . 6–8, 23, 43, 47

Corniani, G. . . . 42, 84–5

Cristoforis, G. B. de . 141–2

Denina, C. 20, 33

Ducis, J. F. 39, 46, 79, 81, 106

Duse, Eleonora . . . 81, 161

Fabbri, Ed. 147–8

Federici, C. 67–8

Foppa, ... 82

Foscolo, Ugo 32, 35, 78, 84, 89–90, 116–7, 127

Gamerra, G. de . 31, 68, 89

Garibaldi, G. 157

Garrick, D. . . . 49, 56, 60

Gherardini, G. . . 101, 123

Giordani, P. 102–3

Goldoni, C. 13–4, 35–8, 39, 40, 47, 153

Golt, G. 93

Gozzi, C. 38–9, 153

N

Gray, T. 34, 60, 73, 84, 96
Grimaldi, R. 24
Gritti, F. 79
Gualtieri, L. 159–60

Jean, ... 136
Johnson, S. 11, 17, 46, 49, 53, 55, 84, 93, 120, 123, 124, 153

Lamberti, L. 68
La Place, P. A. de 39, 41, 57
Leoni, M. 69, 90, 92, 95, 99, 100, 101, 120, 121, 122, 123, 124, 125, 134, 135, 136, 137, 155
Leopardi, G. 101–2
Le Tourneur, P. F. 48, 49, 69, 77, 88, 92, 103, 105, 116, 121, 125, 135
Liruti, A. 64
Lugnani, G. 106–7, 109, 111

Macpherson's Ossian, 34, 64, 84, 101, 126
Maffei, S. . . 11, 27, 34, 47
Magalotti, L. 3
Maldonati, G. 82
Manzoni, Aless. 69, 88, 111–9, 122, 125, 139, 140, 141, 148, 150, 151
Marenco, C. 46, 140, 143, 144–6
Marenco, V. 26
Marescalchi, L. 82
Martinelli, V. 56–7
Mazza, A. 35

Mazzini, G. 132, 133, 135, 160
Meneghelli, P. . . 65–6, 129
Metastasio, P. 11–3, 36, 47, 93
Milizia, F. 24–5
Milton, J. 3, 9, 19, 33, 34, 60, 91, 101, 102, 127, 129
Modena, G. 152–4
Montagu, Elisabeth 48, 55, 58, 59, 60, 61, 132
Monti, V. 34, 69–73, 76, 80, 83, 84, 88, 118
Morelli, A. 154

Napoli-Signorelli, P. . 25–6
Nicolini, Giambattista 148–50, 154
Nicolini, Gius. . . 134, 136
Novelli, E. 161

Pagani-Cesa, G. U. 127–31
Paradisi, A. 24
Pellico, S. 103, 104, 105, 132, 142–3
Pepoli, A. 38, 67
Pignotti, L. 58–61
Pindemonte, G. 74–6, 90–2
Pindemonte, S. 73–4
Ponte, L. da 80, 82
Pope, A. 34, 59, 60, 74, 101, 123, 128, 129

Quadrio, F. 19–20

Ramirez, G. 81
Renier-Michiel, G. . . 76–8

Riccardi, A. 126
Riccoboni, L. 20
Richeri, L. 27
Ristori, A. . . 155, 159, 161

Roberti, G. 23
Rolli, P. 9–10
Rossi, E. 152, 154–8, 159, 160
Rowe, N. 77, 120
Rusconi, C. 136, 154, 155, 159, 163

Salfi, ... 84
Salvini, A. M. 40
Salvini, G. 161
Salvini, T. 142, 152, 158–9
San-Severino, ... 81
Sanctis, F. de 133
Schiller, J. 88, 101, 105, 131, 140, 141, 147, 152
Schlegel, A. W. von 54, 88, 99, 100, 105, 118, 120, 123, 129, 130
Shakespeare's Plays :—
  All's Well That End's Well, 97
  Antony and Cleopatra, 22, 27, 116, 119, 124
  As You Like It, . . 73, 97
  Comedy of Errors, . 82, 83
  Coriolanus, 72, 145, 157; Translations, 76, 77, 135
  Cymbeline, 145; Translation, 120
  Hamlet, 4–5, 16, 20, 22, 23, 28, 42, 47, 49, 51,

52, 57, 58, 60, 70, 72, 76, 79, 80, 82, 83, 88, 89, 95, 96, 108, 116, 117, 126, 132, 145, 146, 151, 153, 154, 155–6, 157, 158, 159–60, 161, 162, 163, 164 ; Translations, 77, 120, 136
  Henry IV, 9, 51, 72, 86, 97, 109, 114, 119 ; Translation, 120
  Henry V, ... 87
  Henry VI, ... 23, 60
  Henry VIII, 64, 70, 71, 86, 114, 116 ; Translation, 136
  Julius Cæsar, 6, 7, 8, 17, 18, 19, 22, 24, 27, 28, 29, 58, 59, 60, 69, 71, 72, 74, 86, 88, 109, 111, 115, 118, 124, 145, 158, 161 ; Translations, 39, 41–3, 57, 92–4, 118, 120, 121, 134, 136, 158
  King John, Translation, 120
  King Lear, 157, 161, 164 ; Translations, 120, 134, 136
  Macbeth, 10, 24, 28, 45, 46, 49, 75, 86, 90, 95, 104, 106–7, 112, 114, 117, 118, 123, 124, 125, 126, 130, 145, 149, 151, 157 ; Translations, 76, 77, 120, 134, 136
  Measure for Measure, 67, 161

Merchant of Venice, 157, 161; Translation, 136

Merry Wives of Windsor, 36

Midsummer Night's Dream, 36, 60, 161; Translations, 120, 134, 137–8

Much Ado About Nothing, 161

Othello, 9, 16, 20, 28, 57, 59, 71, 89, 92, 103, 104, 108, 112, 114, 117, 124, 125, 126, 130, 143, 144, 146, 151–4, 155, 158, 161, 162, 164; Translations, 76, 77, 120, 134, 135, 136

Richard II, 112–4; Translation, 120

Richard III, 9, 45, 60, 86, 109–11, 114, 117, 146, 149, 155, 163; Translations, 120, 136

Romeo and Juliet, 45, 56, 58, 75, 80, 81, 82, 99, 117, 122, 125, 151, 157, 159, 161, 164; Translations, 120, 134, 136

Taming of the Shrew, 161

Tempest, 49, 60, 104, 117, 125, 161; Translations, 120, 134, 136, 137

Timon of Athens, . . . 116

Titus Andronicus, . . . 23

Troilus and Cressida, . . 87

Winter's Tale, ... 161

Sheffield, John, Duke of Buckinghamshire, . . . 6, 7, 8

Sherlock, M. . . . 17–8, 28

Sismondi, J. C. L. 64, 105, 127

Sornani, G. 134

Spinelli, G. Carrara . 126–7

Stael, Mme. de 80, 88, 98–101 102, 117, 127, 131

Tedaldi-Fores, C. 88, 139, 140, 147

Tommaseo, N. 104

Torti, G. 104, 119

Valentini, D. 39–40, 41–3, 57, 63

Valle, C. della 142

Valletta, I. 118

Veronese, A. 40–1

Verri, A. . . 31, 32, 43, 55–8

Verri, P. 31, 33, 57

Viganò, S. 152

Visconti, E. . 104, 119, 130

Voltaire, F. M. Arouet de 15– 18, 19, 20, 23, 24, 27, 29, 31, 33, 34, 39, 41, 47, 48–55, 57, 62, 70, 102, 108, 112, 119, 120, 125, 158

Young, E. . 27, 34, 84, 90

Zacconi, E. 161

Zeno, A. 4

DATE DUE